Tie Me, Tie You!

BONDAGE IN THE BEDROOM

Tie Me, Tie You!
Bondage in the Bedroom

A FULLY ILLUSTRATED REPORT ON THE POPULARITY OF
CONSENSUAL "LOVE BONDAGE" AS A SEXUAL TURN ON
FOR MEN & WOMEN

By Robert Q. Harmon

HARMONY PUBLICATIONS INC.
LOS ANGELES,, CALFORNIA

ISBN 13:
978-0-692-85676-5

AN IMPORTANT NOTE
TO OUR READERS

This book is an informative and occasionally entertaining report on a sub-culture. It is not intended to promote bondage nor does it advocate that readers experiment. On the contrary, *these activities are probably not for you and should not be tried!*

But in the event that you do...

USE CAUTION - USE DISCRETION - USE DUE DILIGENCE - USE COMMON SENSE!

We urge you to take care in choosing your bondage partners. **We strongly recommend that if you do play bondage, be absolutely certain that it's with someone you trust, someone who offers no danger to you - so much the better if it's someone you love who loves you.**

Because you are putting yourself completely at another person's mercy - potentially the most dangerous thing you've ever done.

And, if you dabble in self-bondage, best have someone nearby or a way of signaling someone who can help you out of whatever predicament you've constructed. And do not put rope or other material on your own or anyone else's neck.

And now, with that regard for safety sealed firmly in the forefront of our minds, let's start turning pages and finding out about all this.

Contents

ABOUT "BONDAGE LIFE," THE PUBLICATION FROM WHICH MOST OF THE MATERIAL IN THIS BOOK IS DRAWN:

Since 1978, Bondage Life has been generally accepted in the bondage community as the best publication ever. There has certainly never been any other publication like it in the American bondage scene.

The format is an original one for the bondage field, that of a national newsmagazine. Using this non-fictionalized compartmentalized documentary approach, Bondage Life has gleaned bondage lore from every aspect of society and presented it in a style of journalistic objectivity.

In describing the impact Bondage Life has made, people tend to use words like "elevating" and "uplifting." The contents of Bondage Life make people nod knowingly: "Yes, this is for us; this is our thing. They know who they're talking to. This is wonderful. It's so clean and openly unashamed."

Bondage Life declared itself as the magazine "For and By Bondage People." It published its 85th and final issue in 2003.

—ALLEN MARBURGER
"BONDAGE ENTERTAINMENT IN
MODERN MEDIA"

*"Okay, Honey, you can untie me, but
be slow about it!"*

-BONDAGE MODEL JENNIFER WEST

PART ONE
The What and Who of It

"Heart to heart
lips to lips
We're chained and bound
Together..."

"You're Mine You"
Johnny Green & Edward Heyman 1931

Somewhere, a woman is stretched out on a bed. Her wrists are tied. So are her ankles. And the gag around her mouth prevents her from speaking. She is helpless, unable to move. Totally at the mercy of whomever placed her in that situation.

And she's enjoying every weird second of it.

Because this woman is one of the many active practitioners of so called consensual "Love Bondage," which she and probable millions of others have adopted as an exciting offbeat prelude to lovemaking. And it is possible that the man or woman in the room with her is recording this scene on videotape for inclusion into their beloved collection of private bondage videos.

Elsewhere, similar scenes of bondage are also being filmed or videotaped—some for personal pleasure, some for profit. What is intensely an intimate activity between lovers has been discovered and lapped up by sharp-eyed commercial profiteers. Videos, films, magazines, books and websites depicting bondage activities sprout like weeds after the rain. It may be fairly said that the bondage business is booming.

My name is Robert Q. Harmon and I happen to be one of those merchants. Have been for close to 40 years. With that, and given all the letters I've received during those years, all the stories I've been told, all the pictures I've been sent, I'm probably better suited than anyone to tell the full story of the bondage phenomenon.

•

The imprint begins early, in the formative years, when a casual bondage scene from a motion picture or a picture in a magazine imprints itself favorably and for who knows what reason into that part of the brain where sexual interest resides. That scene will resonate pleasurably in that person's mind forever more, and he, or she, will spend significant parts of their lifetimes trying to duplicate it in whatever ways are possible.

Because, from that impressionable first moment forward, the sight of an attractive woman bound and gagged becomes the essential central ingredient in his or her tableau of imagined sexual pleasures—the situation he or she most longs to see or actually experience.

The why of that is yet unknown, but theories abound— as diverse as snowflakes and fingerprints. The most oft-spouted theory is that it's the rescue fantasy that's in play here—he saves the damsel from her distress and is rewarded eternally with her unconditional love. Were it only that simple because the truth is, no one knows for sure why bondage is the root passion of so many people. Maybe no one ever will. Maybe the why of it doesn't even matter.

•

SPLASHING DOWN INTO THE MAINSTREAM—FOR A WHILE

It took a couple of unlikely and utterly dissimilar gents to prod bondage for pleasure (and profit) into its earliest mainstream appearances. Before Irving Klaw and John Willie, bondage was generally thought of as a criminal act between villains and victims. No one, except its understandably closeted advocates, saw it as a kinky sexual diversion. Even renowned sexual scholars Havelock Ellis and Richard von Krafft-Ebing failed a single mention of it in their weighty compendiums of offbeat sexual practices.

So bondage as a sexual activity was a deep secret best kept to those drawn to it. It just wasn't talked about or written about.

Eventually, the concatenation of a Manhattan pinup photo merchant and a prodigal English seaman and a pert free-as-you-please Tennessee brunette nudged bondage into its first public focus. These three otherwise unnoted individuals planted the first seeds of what eventually would be a thriving cultural harvest and pretty good business model to boot.

Irving Klaw was a downtown Manhattan retail and mail order merchant of movie stills who did not fail to notice that the photo scenes he was selling of leading ladies tied up were outselling everything else. In particular, Veronica Lake all trussed up in "This Gun for Hire!" and

Virginia Mayo bound and gagged in "The Secret Life of Walter Mitty" rode highest atop the charts. Runners up included Maureen O'Hara, Anne Jeffries, Jane Greer, the oft-immobilized girl from the Saturday morning "Sky King" television serial and others.

One of Klaw's steadiest customers - a prosperous New York lawyer - prevailed on Klaw to hire models and pose them in bondage. In return for a single copy of each picture Klaw produced, the lawyer would pay all model, photographer and processing fees. All proceeds, great or small, would accrue to Klaw.

Klaw promoted his bondage photo sets in girlie magazines and orders immediately flooded in. At that point, Klaw undoubtedly beheld a vision of great eventual wealth flowing his way.

Meanwhile, John Willie, a witty but outcast merchant seaman thought to have descended from a reputable English banking company, was going roundabout to New York from England via Australia and Canada. Willie liked to draw, which he did beautifully. And what he liked to draw most were pretty women who were tied up.

Willie eventually landed, hat and samples in hand, in Irving Klaw's 14th Street office whereupon he was rewarded with a commission to draw a sexy cartoon serial to be published in various pinup magazines of the day. What Willie eventually produced — a clever and beautifully drawn bondage serial titled "Sweet Gwendoline" — remains to this day — more than a half-century later — the most beloved artifact in bondage history.

So, there's Klaw and there's Willie. And now, just to make it perfect, who should stride into Klaw's studio to join his other bondage models and to further insure his already skyrocketing success than that best liked, prettiest, still even now reverently-whispered-about shapely little hunk of Tennessee charm who was the most popular pinup model of all

time and whose name was Betty Page.

For bondage, at long last, there in 1950, all the right people had shown up together at the right time. Like the French impressionists of the mid-19th Century or the New York Yankees of 1927. So, for a while there, it was all good.

But, as all of us have been fairly and repeatedly warned, things don't always turn out well and absolutely nothing lasts forever. Irving Klaw was hounded out of business by a self-righteous senate sub-committee and died of peritonitis in 1962. Legal pressures caused Willie to flee to Hollywood to eke out a hand-to-mouth existence. He eventually returned to England in 1962 where he died of a brain tumor at age 60. Betty Page slipped out of public view and was tracked down and found decades later living a reclusive life in a Southern California trailer park. She died in 2010 at age 79.

And, with their passings, the breath of commercial mainstream life they had created for bondage was extinguished. But not forever.

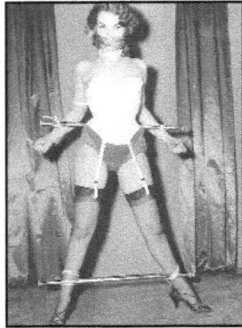

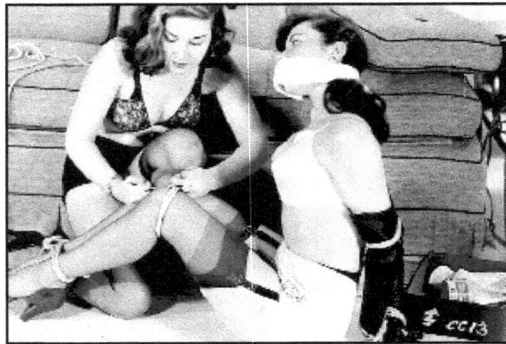

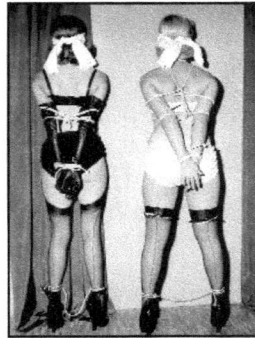

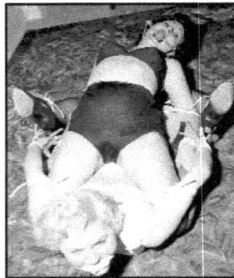

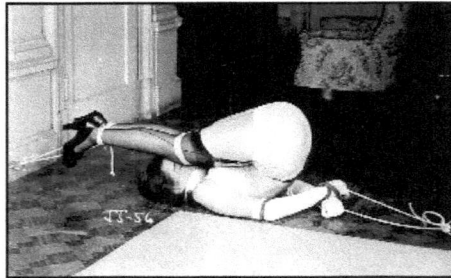

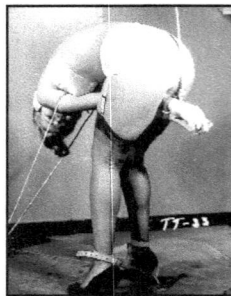

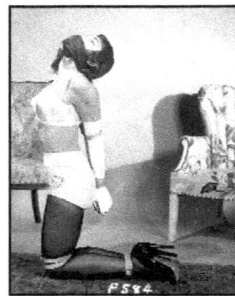

Klaw-ing their way up the ladder of bondage immortality. 50 cents a picture in the 1950's. Irving Klaw produced and sold the first commercial bondage photos.

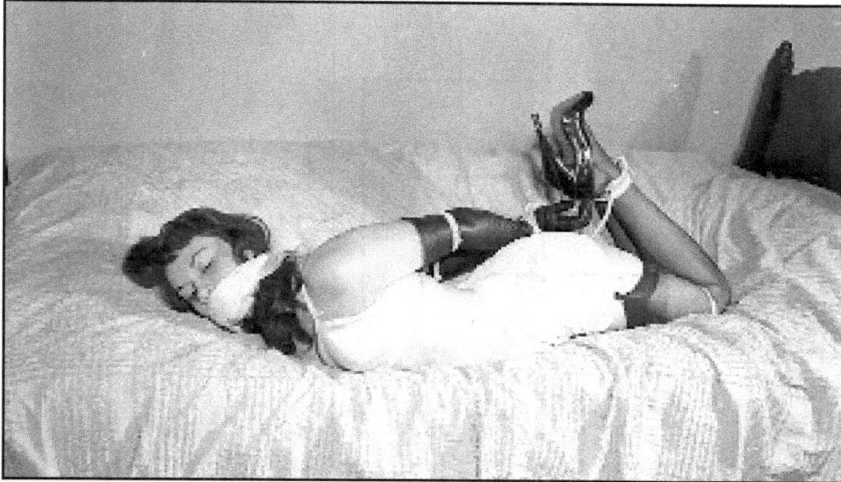

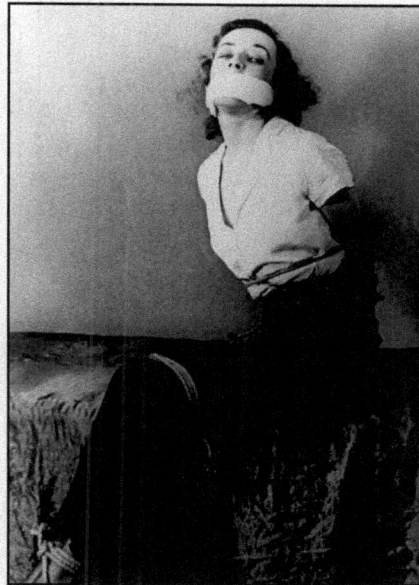

He's the one who started it all. John Willie is considered the progenitor of bondage art—both with his photographs from the 1930's and his artwork, principally his melodramatic "Sweet Gwendoline" cartoon serial. That's Mrs. Willie – "Holly" over on the right.

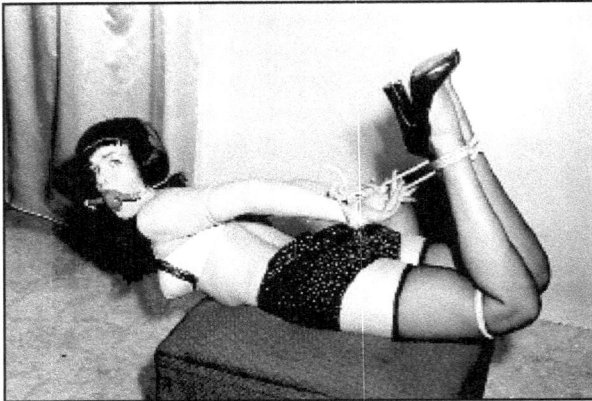

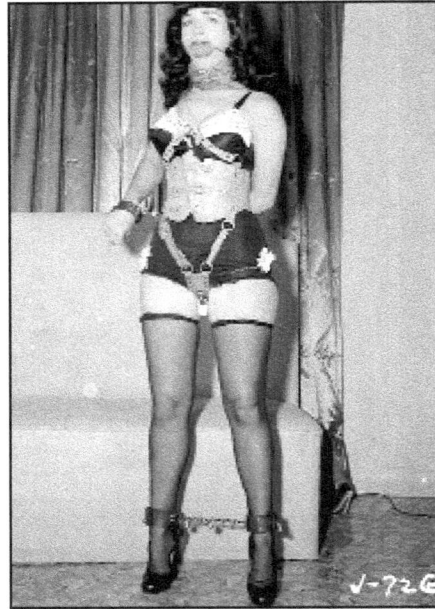

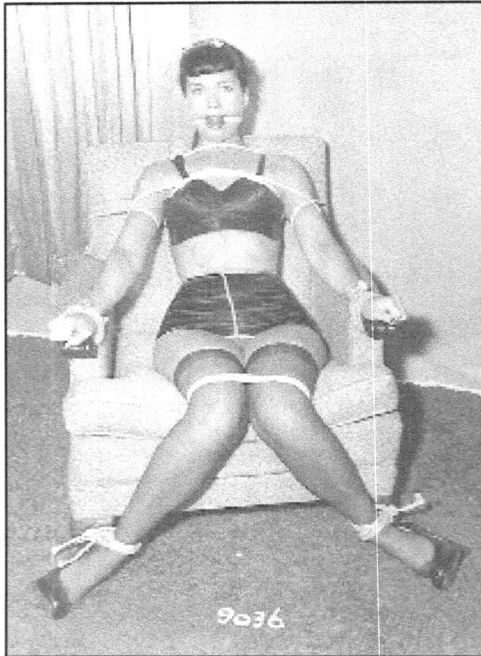

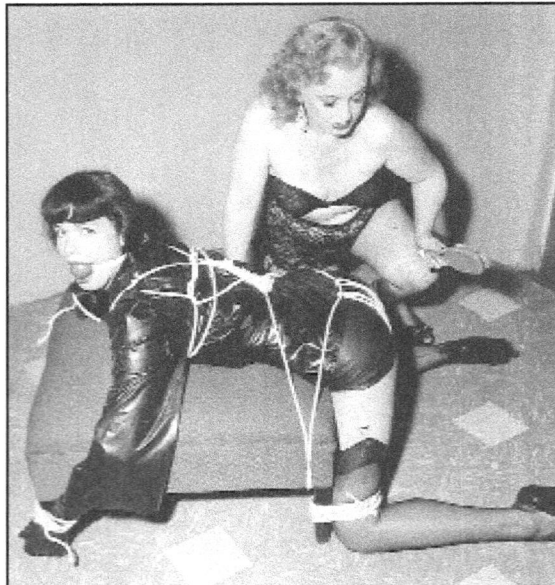

Betty Page – The most beloved bondage model of all time!

NOW HERE'S A WIFE WHO REALLY GETS IT...

My husband is a hard-working marketing executive in a high-stress field. He's a very good man. He worries a lot and that makes me worry for him. We've been married for 11 years and do not have children. We love each other and are each other's best friend.

As for me, I still rate male attention although it's definitely dwindling. I was my high-school's homecoming queen and won a few local beauty contests back in the day and still get hit on from time to time. So it's probably important for these purposes to note that I'm not unattractive.

As a free-lance interior designer, I'm able to choose my own schedule and I occasionally make it a point to be home early in order to create a situation that takes him away from his worries, at least for a while. What we do is spiritually and sexually satisfying to both of us. In fact, it has ratcheted our marriage up from good to great.

Early in our relationship, in a vulnerable moment, he confessed to me that he had always been sexually aroused at the sight of a woman tied up, even as a boy. He was embarrassed about it and never told anyone else. He said any picture in a magazine or scene in a television program that showed a woman bound and gagged had a weirdly pleasant effect on him. But he told me not to worry, he would certainly never impose these desires on me.

A year or so went by with nothing more being said about it, but to me it was that elephant in the room thing. I knew he would do anything for me and I had always wondered what I could do for him, how I might make his life more interesting, more fun. And then one day, there it was—The Answer! Daring, but definitely worth the risk.

So, I finished work on Thursday afternoon and headed home, plan in mind. Showered and dressed myself in some moderately sexy underwear-- black panties and bra, hose with garters, heels. Checked myself out in the mirror, decided against the bra and thought I looked pretty good. Not a knockout, but still hot enough to rate some passing male attention.

I set a glass of wine on a table near the front door, where he wouldn't miss it and laid out about six pieces of paper with arrows pointing toward the bedroom, but the last piece of paper—the one nearest the bed said "I love you."

And now the hard part—how to tie myself up. I'd given this a fair amount of thinking, figuring that just a few turns of rope here and there would be suitable. I also understood that I was risking the most fragile part of his psyche - he might be embarrassed, maybe even offended but, what the hell, sometimes you just have to go for it. It was about my love for him and I had faith that he would understand and accept that.

So I sat at the edge of the bed and tied my ankles together. Made the ropes as neat as I could—looked pretty good. Then the knees, then the thighs. And now the hard part—my upper body. But before that I gagged myself but not really—just took a length of bed sheet that I had scissored out and wrapped about three times around my lower face. I did what I could about my upper body and wrists, not great, but passable. And then relaxed into it and waited. It was so strange. Peaceful, pleasant actually. I felt oddly secure and drifted off into a kind of comfortable twilight half-sleep. It surprised me that I felt so serene. Maybe 40-50 minutes later, I heard the front door open and close. I could tell he had picked up the wine and was walking into the room. I saw how startled he was at the sight of his wife being on a bed bound hand and foot and gagged, dressed only in her underwear.

He just stood there, unmoving—somewhere between bewildered and thrilled. For a few minutes, all he did was stare. Then I began to squirm suggestively, signaling him to settle onto the bed beside me. When he did, I rolled over so that my back was to him. A minute or two clicked by and then, tentatively, shyly, he put his hands on me and began to feel me, and then caress me. Eventually, he gained confidence and took physical charge of me, bringing his head down and kissing me through my gag and putting his arms around me and embracing me like never before. I had never ever felt that level of powerful loving intimacy from him before. Whatever doubts I'd ever had about our being soulmates vanished in those moments.

He started to untie me, but I shook my head against it signaling him to leave me just as I was. So there we were, in this strange yet wonderful moment of our lives—both of us happy knowing that we had somehow achieved a beautiful intimacy. We made tender love and when it was over, he whispered his thanks. We've repeated that special scene several times since, varying it in subtle ways and always careful to not overdo it—trying always to keep it fresh and special.

I've gotten better about tying myself and I've learned that by using a stretchy hood over my head, I can enjoy the sensation of sensory deprivation while I wait for him. He is never eager to consummate and neither am I. Often, we just spend hours cuddling and rubbing against each other, enjoying each other's bodies, delaying our inevitable gratification. But, then, eventually, I feel him enter me and move inside of me while I'm tied and hooded. It is truly the best lovemaking we've ever had and each time seems better than the last.

There is now something between us that only we know about. We look at each other when we're in restaurants and other public places and recognize that we have this delicious secret. And we are very much in love with each other.

I think the point of my letter is to express the loving effect the sight of my bondage has on my husband. And how maybe it can be useful to other couples. To us, it's like catnip to a cat. He is turned on at the sight and I am turned on by the effect my bondage has on him. Neither of us knows or cares why. We just love the "is" of it—the fact that pleasure replaces tension, for both of us. Sex is the eventual payoff, but it's what we are sharing along the way that is most beautiful for us.

Our world, our lives, in those moments is exquisite, perfect.

Barbara in Toronto

BEEN THERE, KINDA LIKED IT...

"You know, I think bondage is a lot more common than anyone knows. I find it's the men who have stressful, stressful jobs who are into this; and they've found this way to release tension. It's a kind of therapy."

BONDAGE MODEL ALLISON BRACH BONDAGE LIFE 71

"I wouldn't just like the act of bondage without any surrounding fantasy. He can dress up like Superman, or wear some costume—a man of mystery. That would be wonderful. I want it to have some drama to it, be a romantic fiction."

BONDAGE MODEL KELSIE CHAMBERS BONDAGE LIFE 71

"...and it was so enjoyable that I just kept asking for bondage modeling assignments."

BONDAGE MODEL STAR CHANDLER BONDAGE LIFE 67

"I never realized what an erotic experience being bound up could be. I thought, well, this feels kind of nice. And the next photo shoot, I was struggling around and thought this is *really* nice! I think fetish, including bondage, is healthy since it's another way to express one's self in a sexual way."

BONDAGE MODEL KELLY ASHTON BONDAGE LIFE 70

"When you're captive, when you're bound, you are the object of attention and affection. You're the center of the universe and that's a wonderful feeling."

BONDAGE MODEL ALEXIS PAYNE BONDAGE LIFE 68

THE MOST STUNNING AND POWERFUL, MOST REMEMBERED SIGHT OF HIS LIFE!

This was probably the first bona-fide bondage photograph to ever appear in a conventional general interest magazine. It was used to illustrate a text piece on fetishism which appeared in the November 1949 issue of "Night and Day," a long-ago postwar publication with no discernible bloodline to a later magazine with the same title.

"It was that first, unfocused hour after school, and I was standing in a drug store thumbing through one of the magazines I always made it a point to look at because it was usually good for a few sports stories and a sexy picture or two.

"Suddenly, this incredible picture of a woman being tied onto a wooden frame came floating off a page and right into my soul and everything inside me was pounding and reeling and an exquisite passion throbbed upward through me like lava.

"She was very pretty. For a minute I even let myself imagine that she was the tight-skirted, blouse-stretching song leader that every guy in the school fell asleep thinking unspeakable things about every night. Whoever she was, I was in immediate love with her.

"I got the feeling that she didn't mind what was being done to her. The partially hidden female behind her, taking such loving care with the tying, also struck me as beautiful and I figured I might as well love her too, since what she was doing there to her friend made me feel absolutely wonderful.

"She had knotted a pretty black gag snugly around her subject's face, and had applied effective twists of cord onto the wrists, arms, ankles,

thighs and around the waist of the seemingly agreeable brunette. Those few strands of rope might just as well have been strands of solid steel, so irrevocable was the bondage. Our intriguing song leader was there to stay.

"Her wardrobe had the same surging effect on me as the bonds which immobilized her—high heel black leather boots laced up to slightly below her knees, and black, shiny gloves stretched down to her shoulders. She wore a white pointy bra and white panties which had been secured high on her waist and locked by the rope there. I couldn't imagine anyone being more fetchingly dressed for the occasion.

"Whether she liked it or not, she was tightly tied in an inviting spread-eagle pose—a vision of loveliness vulnerable to any sexual possibility.

"In the mind-splitting first instant that I saw that picture and felt all that raw pleasure surging through my senses, came also the bittersweet realization that it was all too important to me, that, for better or worse, the scene in that picture had an overpowering effect on me and I would want to work bondage into every loving relationship I was to ever have.

"Now, more than twenty-thousand days and nights after having seen it for the first time, I still think it is the most perfectly composed and representative bondage photograph I have ever seen."

G.F., Anaheim, Calif

THEY'D FOUND EACH OTHER AND SETTLED
CONTENTEDLY INTO THEIR LONGED-FOR FANTASY LIFE.
THEN HE GOT ON THAT ACCURSED AIRPLANE...

Master Gallery Recalled –
An Interview with Joanne Link

He told her that his first sensual reaction to bondage was brought on by a movie scene at age 14. That had been 24 years before. Since then, bondage had been the principal habit of his existence.

He was attractive, so it was natural and fitting that a succession of attractive female friends would flow through his life, some of whom he pressed into bondage activities. Then he met her and they began living together and, eventually, he showed her all the pictures he had taken of women he had tied up.

Inevitably, he tied her and photographed her and it became the main sweetness of their life together. Then, with all the pictures he had accumulated through his past years and with this wonderful new model to take even more pictures of, he formed a company and began advertising that he had bondage photos for sale.

She helped him with all this— equal partner whose job it was to be tied up and photographed, process film, write letters, mail envelopes and make deposits, support their newborn enterprise to the best of her energies.

By their third year together, they had a national following and the girl — Joanne Link — was probably a better-known contemporary bondage model than any other. Life was good—their business was growing and tomorrow felt warm to their trusting touch and he got on an airplane one afternoon in March and she was stepping into the shower and the phone rang and she went back and picked it up and the floor began swaying under her and the newspaper reporter's questions about the big Chicago airplane crash and how well had she known him were shrieking out of the phone at her and she pushed it away because now it was a weapon that kept trying to strike at her.

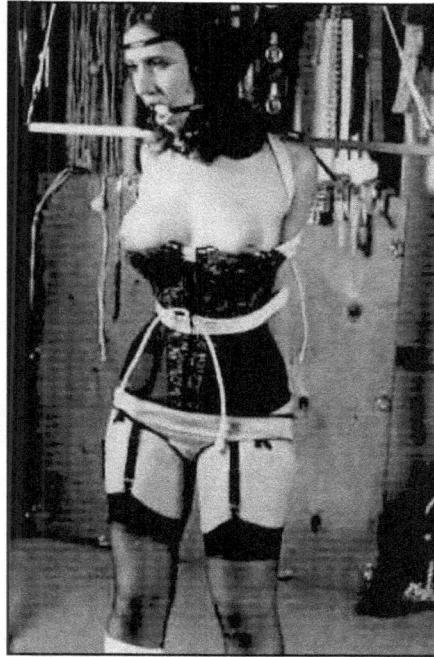

Then, her innocence and faith thus shredded in that insane and awful first sample of human loss, the floor suddenly tilted and she began falling toward it.

You are Joanne Link?

Yes.

To set the stage for this, I read about you and Master Gallery about two years ago—a favorable tabloid article profiling the bondage photos you had for sale.

That was our first big publicity break.

Hundreds of responses, I would think.

More like thousands. Mostly for bondage photos, but requests for other situations too.

Then, last year, we produced The Bondage Buyers Guide & Almanac and most of the people who wrote to us said they liked your pictures best.

Well, that tabloid article you saw did bring us a lot of customers and it looked like we were really on our way.

Then Jay Wells was killed and it was over- just like that.

Yes.

That happened last March, slightly more than a year ago. And you've been out there somewhere ever since. What has it been like for you?

It isn't a year I would want to live over. I think I've been sad. I know I am a little more withdrawn now. If my life with Jay would have been more conventional, then maybe things would be different now.

That means the life you once had with him has had some residual effect on the one you're living now.

Well, here I am talking to you. That would not have happened had Jay not been into bondage because that is what you are interested in. The hardest part after Jay died is that there wasn't anyone I could talk to about the kind of life we led. Not too many people I knew would have understood, so it wasn't something I could share with other people. People with more conventional life styles can go back and discuss their pasts even with strangers. But our life was so totally devoted to bondage that there isn't too much else to talk about. Aside from that, a lot of people don't know even now that Jay was killed and they keep mailing in orders. This interview with you. . . this is the first time anybody will have come out and said, "Hey, Jay is gone. . . there are no new pictures." I still have some material around, so I do try to fill whatever orders I can and I tell these people about what did happen to Jay. I think they de-

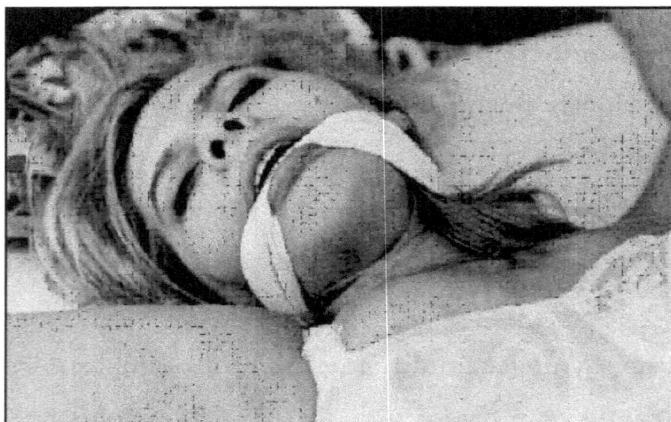

serve some kind of answer.

He liked bondage and he was a photographer to boot. So he ties up female friends and take their pictures like that, as a hobby for his own pleasure.

Yes, but even before he decided to go all out and turn it into a business, he had been in touch with other people who were into bondage and who offered to buy his pictures. So going into it as strongly as he did was just a natural step. He loved it and he knew what he was doing. I think one of the reasons his pictures were so popular is that he didn't worry about the model's comfort or how she felt about him. He was too good a photographer for that, too professional. Too many photographers worry too much about how the model feels and the picture shows it. The last think bondage modeling can possibly be is comfortable, because then it would be obviously unrealistic.

True, that point gets driven home to us a bit more every time we shoot a new bondage scene. At first, we were overly solicitous of our models' comfort and it just doesn't work. Bondage is not the proper medium for such personal consideration. If she is not really tied, it shows up in the picture plain as day and what you have is a lousy picture no matter how good everything else is.

Well, if you're going to do it, give it everything you've got and I'm speaking as much about the model as the photographer. Maybe you should let her know up front exactly what poses you want and what it will probably be like. That way, she knows what she is getting into and she'll even have a better idea of what to do to help make the pictures better. The responsibility becomes less one-sided.

Okay, to you now. Here was a company, Master Gallery of Detroit —one man really, looming up out of nowhere and attracting national bondage attention, a modern day Irving Klaw. And here you are, an ordinary girl, not too many years out of high school, cast as a principal of that company–model, clerk-typist, bookkeeper, consultant in the business, partner. How did all that come to pass?

Truth?

Please.

I met a fellow... it was at a wedding and we dated. The second time we were together, he asked me if I had ever heard of bondage. I didn't have any idea of what he meant. He said it was a form of sexual activity, tying women up. A month later, we were living together and I was getting curious about it.

Had he told you that he personally enjoyed this as a sexual diversion?

Yes. He had decided after several difficult experiences with women who were shocked either when he told them about bondage or when they accidentally saw some pictures around the house. Well, he figured the best thing to do was tell me right off the bat. He said he felt so strongly about it that he wanted to live that way. He wanted to say it and be done with it,

30

not waste time.

What was your reaction about being the one he was telling these odd personal things to?

I liked him. I don't think I was shocked. And I was young and not set in my own ways like some of the women he had known.

It must have struck you as unusual, this fondness he had for tying women up. Were you able to grasp what he saw in it?

I had to see pictures. I think the only reason I did understand was that during one of our "scenes" together, I related to an incident which had happened to me when I was about five and hadn't thought about since. After seeing a movie where they tied up the main actress and put her in the trunk of a car—it might have been "The Purple Gang" or one of those movies — I remember getting a sexual turn-on. I don't know what it was because you bury those things. I had forgotten about it until this particular session with Jay. He kept asking me questions about it— wanting to hear more and more. Another time, I was maybe six or seven, I tied a rope. . . curtain-rod, around my ankles and pulled them up and above me and then the rope broke. I was embarrassed, I tried to hide the curtain rod...just bury it. All your life, you hear this is bad and that is bad and you just bury these things. I never thought of it again until that night with Jay.

You're out in a car with a man you are dating for the second time and he makes what amounts to a confession. He likes you or he wouldn't be telling you this, it's too personal. Did-

n't you immediately recognize that you were being set up to play the female lead in this fantasy of his?

I was awfully impressed with his honesty and that is what struck me the most. And he waited for at least a month before making any attempt at bringing bondage into our relationship. It was appealing that he held back. He talked about it all the time, and there I was wondering if he was ever going to bring it into our relationship.

Your appetite was being whetted, maybe?

Yes, that is what he was doing.

How did he finally get around to asking you?

I asked him. Because I had seen all the pictures of his past girl-friends. I wanted him to be able to enjoy me at least as much as he had them.

Was he shy the first time you finally got into it?

Not at all. He was very positive, he took charge. Maybe it had to be so I would ask him so that there would not be any chance of rejection.

Did you ever feel you were in any kind of danger?

A few times, yes.

Really?

He would get so involved that I would worry about him getting carried away.

How might that have happened?

Suspension maybe. I was paranoid about little things that most people probably don't even think about -- the hook in the wall supporting all my weight might pull out and I would fall. In fact, one time when I was being lifted up onto a table, I did fall. There wasn't any way I could catch myself and I came down real hard on my shoulder. That's when I saw that if anything ever did go wrong, it might not look like an accident and Jay would be in serious trouble.

So did you try and hold him in check?

We had signals. . . sometimes I would even cry. He would always stop.

Joanne, you've had letters – hundreds or thousands or whatever. And these letters are little more than confessions of their writers' deepest psychological secrets.

Yes.

Alright, then maybe from these letters you've learned answers to some questions which aim themselves dead center into the bondage psyche. For example, I've heard all kinds of opinions about what it is that causes bondage to have a powerful sensual effect on men and women. Surely, based on what you've learned from all the letters you've gotten, you've managed to form some kind of opinion – what is it that causes this man or that man to become so inflamed by the sight of a bound and gagged female?

Well, it gets deep and there really is no single answer any more than there is no uniform bondage situation that appeals to all. With Jay, it resulted from a very dominating mother—they have such an effect on children. Maybe it causes a subtle anger inside him which caused him to want to get back at all women — to degrade them, to control them. Jay had these characteristics. From my own point of view, I think I managed to enjoy bondage because I had no control over the situation once I was bound up and helpless and so I didn't have to feel guilty.

The "It's a sin to enjoy sex" Catholic girl syndrome?

I think so. In fact, I went to a Catholic school and they made sex black as night. Now, I think that is ridiculous, but there isn't anything you can do when you are living in that influence. You can't enjoy sex, you aren't supposed to, so maybe the best thing is to be tied up and taken, made to submit. That way, you can't really be guilty of anything — it's happening against your will.

Let me tell you some of the concepts I've heard and you can either confirm or dispel them. One is that the male bondage lover is nothing more than a guy who isn't able to get women to cooperate with him. So he captures them, ties them up and has his way because they aren't in any position to oppose him.

No, no. I know of several couples with terrific relationships, attractive people who would interest almost anybody romantically. I knew one man...he had a very dominating personality. He could never get into the position of being his own boss. He was in a very structured profession. He wasn't able to get high enough. His wife, a beautiful woman, treated him like a king. He needed that... he needed to feel he was really something and she could give him that. He loved it. He could be the boss with her, but not out there in the world.

Was he attractive?

Very.

...so he wasn't someone who needed to force a woman to do anything. He could have his share, pick of the litter and all that, on just his looks or attitude....

It's only a problem when a woman doesn't accept it. Her man's sexual personality isn't necessarily what he shows to the world. It's just what he does privately, and it has nothing to do with the way he acts otherwise. If a woman would submit and do whatever it is he wants, he would probably reward her a hundredfold. It isn't that big a deal—there can at least be compromise here since there will have to be in the other aspects of their relationship or the whole thing will fail.

What is the most unusual request you've ever had, through the mail or otherwise?

One man wanted me to pose specifically for him in red galoshes, the old type, and a fur-collared wraparound coat. It had to be a certain length. The picture had to be an outdoors scene. And the position he wanted me in was for me. . . impossible. I would have had to be double-jointed in every way. He wanted me to put my arms around my ankles, twice. That was one. There were others. He sketched them out so I would have it right.

Maybe he was putting you on.

Possibly, but I find very little of that in this. I thought he was strange.

Do any of these people frighten you?

At first, some did. I got used to it. There is a pattern — the stranger the request, the more submissive the writer seems to be. I get the feeling that what they really want is to have this done to them.

What was the most commonly requested bondage position from people who ordered your pictures?

Spread-eagled.

Did your customers insist that the model be gagged?

Most of them did prefer that. Now I have to say something here. . . I think people who are involved in frequent bondage situations should have signals just in case anything hurts too much or starts to go wrong. We had signals and I think it is a good idea.

What about being blindfolded?

Not being able to see is intriguing. Being tied up by someone you

35

love and not being able to see what he is doing has something going for it.

Was there ever anything you did in bondage that was more exciting than other things? Were you ever carted off to the mountains blindfolded?

Once my boyfriend and one of his friends blindfolded me and put me inside the van. They tied me up and told we were all going to a bondage party where I would be introduced. They played it up very big and I believed it because we drove for a very long time and I didn't hear any sounds that were familiar. I thought we had gone to another city. Anyway, they got me out of the van and we walked around for a while and finally into some house. I was still blindfolded. I thought it was really exciting to be going around like that outside.

How were you dressed?

In stockings and corselet. But I had clothes on over these. My hands were tied behind my back

With rope?

Handcuffs. Since I was blindfolded I had no idea of where I was, or who was watching, anything. Actually, I thought the police were going to show up, which would have been very embarrassing. They kept telling me to keep quiet.

Why didn't they just tie a gag in your mouth?

They kept asking me how I felt and they wanted to hear my answers. I got inside this house and it was so quiet that I would have sworn fifty people were there looking at me. They then introduced me. They said, "This is Joanne Link. Turn around, Joanne, show them how you look." I did everything they said, and we started walking downstairs and I heard a radio which was turned on to the station we always listened to and then I knew we were home. After taking off my blindfold and talking about it, they were really turned on because I was so scared and humble. They had me so fooled. That was a lot of fun for us.

You were having an intoxicating effect on your own man and the men who bought your pictures. That must have brought you pleasure.

I was pleased when he was.

Fair enough. How does sadism relate to bondage?

I think bondage is sexual, but that sadism usually isn't—some other emotional psychology is at work. In bondage, there is love; pain isn't the objective. Possession and ownership and the ability of the male to assert himself and his dominion over his woman is more to the point of bondage.

There is a third school of thought suggesting that a great number of the men... this is so male oriented that I have to frame it in these terms. Let me digress. Are there women who like this, who enjoy bondage? I mean, is it a totally male matter?

No, no. As I told you before, there are women who enjoy it for the reason I gave — it gets rid of the guilt feelings which have been forced into them early on. In bondage, they have to submit and their inhibitions go out the window and what choice do they really have but to enjoy this love and sex. It may be in some cases that she is basically submissive and really wants to be defeated... she wants the man to have to work to take her. On the other hand, if she wins and is able to dominate you, then whatever need she has to be superior is satisfied. If they lose, even if they didn't really want to, they are forced to submit which may be essentially sexual for them. But that's only an opinion which I haven't really worked out yet.

I grew up liking bondage. What I liked... I don't think I was threatened by women and I don't think I was interested in pos-

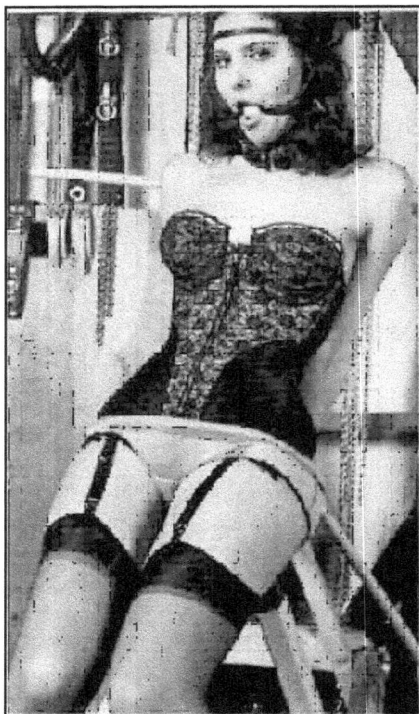

sessing them. While this is not about me, I do wonder about my own attitudes. Somehow it just seemed pretty to me, nothing much more than that. Does that make sense?

You mean the humble, submissive expressions on their faces?

No, I didn't want her to be humble or submissive. And I certainly did not want her to be in any kind of pain. What I did want was for it to be enjoyable for both of us, that we were doing something terribly personal and different with each other. Maybe it brought us as close together as a man and a woman can come.

Sorry, but I think you're in the minority. The men I know want the women in bondage to be frightened, or at least unhappy about her plight.

I want them to be happy about being tied up. I want them to want it. Anyway, there is still that other school of thought which claims that a man who takes pleasure from pictures of women tied and gagged is really fantasizing about how good that would be if it was happening to him, even the way she is dressed. It has nothing to do with being homosexual, or a transvestite or a masochist. He just wants to be at the sexual mercy of a beautiful woman who humiliates him this way, which strikes me as a reasonably heterosexual drive.

Yes, I agree about that. Men sometimes write in posing as a woman, so I understand that some must put themselves in the women's role before they can even talk about it. They write in saying they would like to be dominated, what is it all about? They write back and forth. The first few times, I write back and explain what I can, then they write back again. So it really isn't answers they are after, it is contact — touch and keep in touch and some voyeurism tossed in. They are content to play out their fantasies in the mail because something prevents them from being able to come right out and say, I'm a man, come and tie me up. So they pose as women. One of the problems which stems from this is that some of them actually advertise themselves as bondage loving females in personal sections of newspapers. They send their ad in with a picture of some woman tied up. They identify themselves as that woman. Well, they do get a lot of letters which is what they want, but it's at the expense of sincere people who thought they were writing to an attractive female who shared their interest in bondage relationships.

How many times do you think you have been tied up in your life?

Oh. . .

Eighty-eight? Thirty-four? Six hundred and eight?

No - thousands.

Thousands? Do you have any idea of how many times that is?

Well. . . after three years.

Still, that would be once a day.

Then figure it that way. Figure a thousand times. Sometimes, he would keep me tied up all night.

Would he make love to you?

Yes.

Did you like that?

Depending on the time. No, anything that pleased him pleased me too.

Was there any bondage position you considered your least favorite?

Yes, I've always been conscious of my behind. I think it's too big, even though some writers like that. But I didn't like having to touch my toes. I felt that was the most humiliating position. But there were times when something could be humiliating and exciting at the same time.

What was your favorite position?

Spread-eagled . . . and blindfolded.

Because it is sexy or comfortable?

Because it makes you so vulnerable.

Did he put vibrators in you when he had you tied up?

Once in a while.

Would he turn them on?

Yes, and there was one time when we went to a bar and I had a vibrator inside me and Jay had a remote control for it.

Did he try to bring you to orgasm?

Yes.

Successfully?

Well, when the bar was dark and I could let myself go, yes.

Did you ever enjoy that?

I enjoyed it one time when we went to a theater and he inserted a dildo inside me—it was exciting to know that nobody else knew what we were doing.

There are a lot of bathing caps being worn by Master Gallery's models. I've never seen that before.

I think he used them because they were so humiliating. That was the appeal — with me, the more humiliated I became, the more submissive. That's what he liked.

Joanne, one wonders. There you sit, with a better handle than anyone on a couple of thousand psyches. You're bright, surely you understand that you are getting the darkest parts of these souls handed to you on paper.

I disagree. These are not unacceptable things, so it isn't that big a deal. I do understand the attraction of bondage and that is what most people correspond with me about. But other things, not related to bondage, I think. . . I would rather walk over nails.

Good, because J.B. of Gila Monster, Nevada, writes that he'd like a picture of you walking over a bed of nails.

You and J.B. can both go soak your heads.

Okay, do you find any of your writers interesting?

Some. I'm always impressed when I hear from a doctor, a minister, a teacher. Such people make me feel this is completely acceptable.

If you got a letter tomorrow from a man in Boise, Idaho, offering to pay you handsomely to come there and tie him up. . . in a dress or a man's suit, would you accept?

No, I've had that sort of offer from someone who lived three blocks away, naturally, he didn't know where I lived. Anyway, I didn't accept. You have to understand — this wasn't my thing, it was Jay's. And because I cared about him, I cared about this. I would probably find it very difficult if I didn't care about the person who wanted me to do these things. I respect money, but it wouldn't make any difference as far as this is concerned.

So you don't capitalize on this.

I have.

How?

Posing. A lot of women are not able to let their elbows be tied tightly together and it is a favorite look in bondage. If the elbows are pulled together and then tied like that, it completes the picture in much the same way that a punctuation mark completes a sentence. I can let my elbows be drawn together tightly and then lashed in that position without any trouble. Because of that, we sold a lot of additional photos.

If a man walked into your life right now and struck you as Mr. Right. . . bells and sirens start clanging like crazy. He is everything you want and he has a consuming passion for bondage. Would that affect you?

It would actually make it a lot easier to tell him about my past life and he would probably enjoy hearing about it. If you are asking how I would feel about him, it wouldn't make any difference. After all, you've loaded your case by saying he is Mr. Right and I'm hearing all those bells and sirens. Well, if this man is that terrific he can walk around the house dressed up like a deep-sea diver and it will be okay with me.

I think you explained that it would be better for one reason because you could talk about your past life with Jay more freely. Otherwise, you would always be on your toes guarding against saying anything at all with a man who did not know about it.

Yes, but there are other considerations. You can get hooked on it after three years.

Then, if you were to become involved in a relationship with someone who didn't know from bondage, you might miss it.

Yes.

Sexually, or the day-to-day living mode?

Sexually. But only for a change once in a while. I don't think I would want it to be as intense this time.

Why do you think all the people who have written us about your work liked it so much?

We had a strong combination of realism and good photography.

Jay wasn't reluctant to tie somebody up as good as they could be tied. He really didn't know any other way. Some of the models he used were women he dated and bondage became part of the relationship. When it did, he took pictures. There were times when I did not enjoy it because of the photography, I would be tied up and gagged with one thought on my mind — why doesn't he put that camera down for once and we can have fun.

So, for three years, you lived in an atmosphere which had bondage as its core.

Yes.

Were you ever involved in a bondage situation with more people than just you and Jay?

Yes. A few were out-of-towners who flew into Detroit and would make time for us. There was even a stewardess who flew in alone from time to time.

You mean she enjoyed bondage?

Yes.

Was she pretty?

Yes, very.

Were you ever in a bondage situation with another girl?

Yes, but we didn't encourage that because there was usually her husband or boyfriend around and eventually he would want us all to go upstairs and get into bed together. We weren't into that.

Well, isn't that the ultimate step in bondage anyway? I think of it as a kind of foreplay or prerequisite to sex.

Not in our case. Often, I would be kept tied up and that had nothing to do with sex. Turn me on, but no intercourse.

But, if your man likes bondage, doesn't it follow that he is simply increasing his sexual appetite by tying you up? Doesn't it

arouse him and doesn't he want to consummate it?

Jay was able to withstand that pressure. There were times when I could tell he was aroused, but he stayed to his priorities The thing I did discover about being restrained like that and having someone trying to arouse you is that you reach so many levels that you would not reach under conventional circumstances. You are kept in a constant state of arousal and you do things more than once.

You are speaking, I think, of orgasm.

Yes. It is surprising how much more you can become turned on when there is no escape. . . your body has no choice but to submit, relax. You can have multiple orgasms. In a straight situation, you come down from the plateau after the first time and you have to start again from the beginning. But, when you're tied up and unable to move or resist, you stay up there until your situation is changed.

You've been contacted by thousands of people because of their interest in bondage and the fact that you were an accessible bondage star, right?

Yes.

And now you are going away from it.

Yes. I suppose. Anyway, it was exciting to share private things that you couldn't just talk to anybody about. Usually, you have to hold these things in, hide them, so being able to talk to people was a refreshing release.

You fall in love next Tuesday...with a man who wants you to tie him up. How would that make you feel?

If that submissiveness carried on through to other aspects of his life, it would be hard to respect him and it probably wouldn't work. I need someone I can lean on, someone who dominates me.

But in your sexual life with him?

I could accept it there. It would be okay, maybe even good. I am all for whatever makes it best. If you are in love and you have whatever it is to make him happy, chances are you are going to be happy too. Look, I believe that if you please the one you love, that person will please you. All life is a compromise. If you don't believe that, you aren't going to make it anyway, whatever your sex life. What I really believe about all of this is that we weren't intended to just rub noses.

Afterward, when the plane that was taking her back to Detroit was airborne, someone asked if it had been a good interview. I shrugged that it had been fine.

The melancholy was that the interview could not be published in a national slick so that more people could know about this woman and the compelling events of her life.

For now, she will slip from view to privately carry these poignant secrets with her and I find that too lonely a conclusion to the sensitivity and love she brought to all of this.

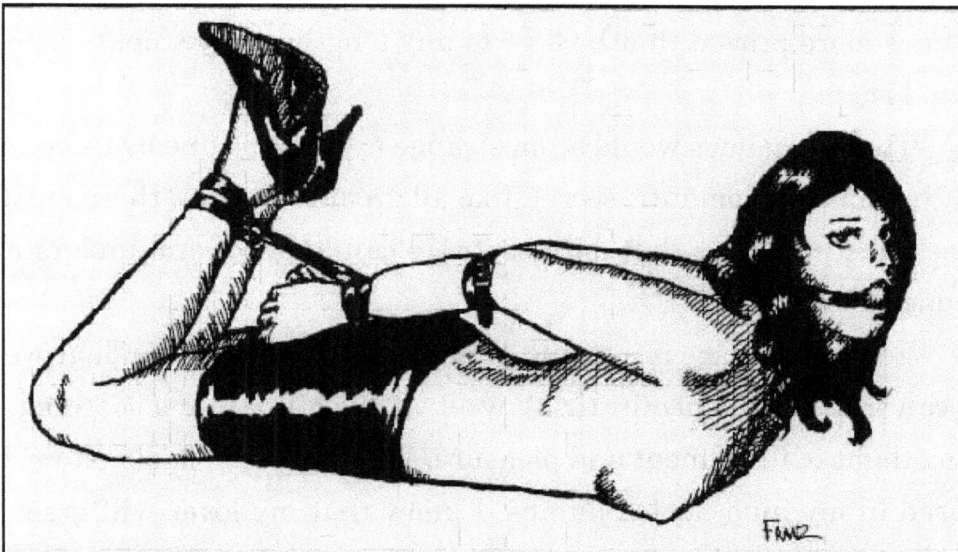

PART TWO
Private Lives - The Imprinted

Bondage is the most romantic game I play with my husband. When bound, I can be whoever I imagine. Sometimes I'm a princess waiting for my prince to save me, other times a captured spy. But no matter what role I choose I know I'll be rescued and loved by the person I love.

Afterward, we draw even closer together because in my mind he has once more proved that he'll go to any length to save me, to be with me, to love me.

That our games would seem strange to others is fine by us because they become our romantic secret; like all great romances, there must be beautiful experiences that only partners can know of and understand. Bondage is ours.

Loving Bondage is exciting, romantic and erotic. A bondage weekend can transform a hectic, tiring week at the office into a soothing, relaxing flight of fulfillment and pleasure. When I return home on Friday, dressed in my high heeled pumps, I know that my lover will greet me and reform me from a weary secretary to his bound fantasy heroine. He likes nothing better than to truss me up in a chair-tie or hog-tie while he prepares dinner. The juices that flow through my body melt away all tensions and anxieties. This is a great way to start a relaxing and loving weekend.

Diane in Detroit

Bondage symbolizes and reinforces the love and respect my wife and I feel for one another. When she is in bondage, she is relying on me to take hold of her emotions so that I can hopefully create new and wonderful feelings for her.

In essence, the rope around her body and the gag over her mouth are symbols of her trust and confidence in me. Because she feels this way toward me, I can't help but love her all the more.

And when I see her in bondage, how can I not think she is more beautiful than ever?

Sincerely, MJK

Bondage is a personal expression of total trust in one's partner. For me, without the trust there would be no bondage.

I was a rather reluctant bondagette in the beginning, when my lover first made his fantasies known to me. It was a major step having that first stocking tied around my wrists, and I'm sure he was afraid that one small stocking would be as far as he would ever get. But as our relationship has grown, so has our bondage experience. I must admit that I now enjoy being quite "trussed up." But the reason I feel free to enjoy myself is because I trust him completely with my body and with my mind. I seldom know what to expect, but I know I won't be hurt or left or laughed at.

Other than trust, the main requirement for a satisfying bondage life is patience by the more daring partner. It's a lot easier to try an unusual experience a little at a time; if my lover had tried to hog-tie and blindfold me the first time we discussed bondage, I doubt that our relationship would be as good as it is. Luckily, he was patient and in the past few years our relationship has become quite interesting to say the least. It often seems a contradiction to me to be a feminist but also to enjoy being bound. The "degradation" aspect was the part that originally bothered me, and probably is what bothers a lot of women. The only thing I can say to that is that if you love and trust and respect each other, a few yards of rope are not going to hurt that relationship.

Sign me, Go For It!

•

HOW AND WHEN IT HAPPENED TO ME

"OH, THOSE SATURDAY AFTERNOON SERIALS DOWN AT THE STRAND!"

CARL MCGUIRE TELLS US ABOUT HIS FIRST SIGHTINGS

Who knows where all our sexual quirks, and tweaks, and bells and whistles come from? We'll never nail that answer down precisely. In my case, though, I can retrieve the memory of a few distinct images from long, long ago that helped hardwire in my brain the idea of female bondage as something potently sexual. Here are two of them:

In the beginning was... the movies. Somewhere around age 10 or 11, I wandered into the Strand Theater for a Saturday afternoon matinee. I don't remember the double feature, but the Strand—like the other kid oriented movie houses in my hometown— showed a serial every weekend, and that Saturday it was a chapter from "Jungle Girl."

Frances Gifford played Nyoka. She was pretty and resourceful and wore a short-skirted buckskin outfit with calf-length boots and swung on vines just like Tarzan, except sexier. I developed an instant crush, and returned for the next few weekends.

Then came the penultimate chapter: Nyoka was tied to a stake by diamond smugglers, a crossbow aimed at her heart, the cord that would

release the arrow stretched over a flame, slowly burning through. At the sight of Nyoka tied there, something happened to me, and the serial wasn't just a diversion anymore but something more profound.

The chapter ended abruptly, and I spent the next week in a kind of daze, knowing something had shifted my world off-center, knowing I would be back in my seat at the Strand the following Saturday, hoping that Nyoka would escape the arrow—but also, paradoxically, hoping she'd never get free.

A couple of years later, as I teetered on the edge of puberty, I was on my way home from school and stopped to browse at the corner newsstand. In the rear was a shelf of girlie magazines—mild by today's standards but pretty titillating back then. I was leafing through something called Gala, which was mostly bathing-suit cheesecake photos of well-endowed dollies, when I suddenly came upon a large ad in the back of the magazine.

It was from Nutrix Corp, Irving Klaw's company, and it consisted of small reproductions of panels from bondage cartoons. All over the page were drawings of gorgeous females bound and gagged in the most bizarre positions. If Nyoka set off a small hand grenade in my psyche, this magazine page amounted to a thermonuclear bomb. Because for the first time I realized that someone made and sold this kind of material, that there must be a market for it, a community of people who enjoyed what I enjoyed. That I wasn't alone.

"THIS IS THE STORY THAT IMPRINTED ME FOREVER!" By Atreus

When it comes to considering the possible sources that have led to a love of bondage – things like movies, television, detective magazines and comic books - we should not overlook one other area that extends back to the early decades of the century, and that in England, Australia, Canada and America parallels and even pre-dates many of the other influences.

These are books we read as youngsters which came to us as birthday and holiday gifts and which may have primed our imaginations for

enjoying the fascinating appeal of bondage.

In story after story, we
hear of chums discovering secret clues to treasure, working to expose smuggling rings
or save a friend who is missing or incriminated in some
nefarious deed. Time and
again we have females being
abducted and kept in
bondage, being rescued by
their friends just in time so
they can rush in and save the day. Often there are unexpectedly stirring
illustrations depicting such moments as well.

There was a strict sexual delineation with these books, whether
they appeared in the thirties or fifties. Rarely did the sexes get to mix in
the adventures. Remember, many of them appeared prior to the en-
lightened sixties, well before the co-educational days of Nancy Drew and
her exploits. Whereas boys were sometimes abducted or captured in the
girls' books, rarely did the reverse happen. A respectable and telling caution prevailed.

There are examples of bondage adventure in these annuals - we
can select several at random that represent both the typical yarn and
the period in which they appeared.

First of all, let's take "Nothing Ever Happens" which was an un-
deniable highlight of The Big Budget for Girls when it was released in
1933. Written by an author who signed himself/herself 'Rusty' (so many
of these female stories were produced by men), this ten-page adventure,

so crisply and knowingly written, gets its three damsels into distress by the end of the second page. Two sisters watch a plane land on a moor, and thinking its two male occupants are having engine trouble, go to see if they can lend a hand (one should never examine the motives in such stories too closely, the main concern is creating the desired situation).

But we hadn't gone more than a dozen yards when we saw something that brought us to a dead stop. In the shadow of a clump of bushes on our right, and almost hidden from sight by the overhanging branches, lay a young woman, huddled up in a fur coat, and as she turned her head we saw that a handkerchief was bound firmly around her mouth.

Jo and Freda managed to untie her ankles and are running with her to safety (she is still gagged, with her hands bound behind her back as an exciting illustration shows). Eventually, they are spotted and pursued by the men.

Overtaken and caught, the sisters are gagged with their own handkerchiefs, bound hand and foot and left lying with the other girl in some bushes while the men return to their business. Jo manages to free her wrists with Freda's assistance and runs off. She later returns to steal the car in which the other girls have been placed and drives down to the nearby village. When the frantic girl pulls up at her house, the language she uses to tell what happened seems designed to get the most mileage it can out of the bondage situations:

I tumbled out of the car, quite incoherent with excitement. "Oh, Father! The men in the aeroplane! They tied us up - and the strange girl – but we've escaped!"

I gasped; and opening the second door of the car I pointed to Freda and the fair-haired girl, who had both been jolted off the seat and sat huddled upon the floor.

" Og-gug-gug! " mumbled Freda, and translating this as a request for freedom to speak, I began to remove the gag.

As for Father - well, he stared at the bound and helpless pair as if he couldn't believe his eyes, and then asked in bewilderment if this was one of our usual pranks.

"Pranks, Daddy!" exclaimed Freda, as soon as her mouth was free. "Why, it's an adventure!" And while I ungagged the strange girl she poured out the story of the afternoon.

It certainly is an adventure, and one wonders what other "pranks" Jo and Freda have gotten up to in the past that make their father so skeptical now. It is interesting too the way that ungagging the fair haired girl is simpler said than done. It is not until right near the end that she is free of her gag and can tell her story.

Another typical example is "Theodora's Bird Man" by Lorna Wood," a later story which appeared in Open-Air Adventure Stories for Girls in 1965, and has the heroine captured by a thief named Papageno and subjected to the classic punishment:

She didn't resist when he pushed her on to the window-seat and

tied her ankles together and then her wrists. . .he sighed and fetched a handkerchief out of his pocket: mercifully, it was a clean one.

Theo gasped: "You're surely not going to gag me – I mean there's no point in it. There's no one around for miles."

"Well, just a minute, then."

"Can't I have a drink before you put that thing on? It's beastly hot."

"And have a crack at me with the bottle? Sorry, not likely."

He put the gag on in an irritatingly expert fashion: you couldn't have said it was torturingly tight but it would obviously take a long time to loosen.

.

Later, her friends come exploring the house where she is held captive and make a startling discovery: as they reached the landing, all three boys froze. They'd seen things like that in the flicks and the TV but never in reality. There stood a girl with hands and ankles tied and a handkerchief in her mouth.

While the description of such bondage is often kept to a minimum, with lines like: "In no time at all, the girls were bound and gagged;" sometimes the mechanics are given and they sound both effective and well-researched.

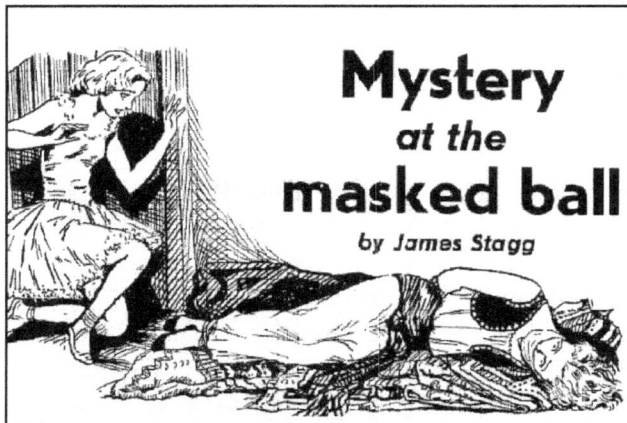

In the story "Ponies All Day Long," which appeared in 1955, Paddy Shane runs afoul of two of your typical villains:

Paddy kicked, wriggled and fought, but the two crooks at last secured her hands behind her back with her school tie and tied her feet together with the girdle of her gym tunic.

There can be no doubt that the British perfected the presentation of these innocent comradely adventures. The stories are characterized by restraint, with the erotic potential so often understated. There is never any overt sexual threat, for instance. The bondage is always employed to incapacitate and delay, to subdue or restrain a nuisance.

Still, the authors of these stories seemed to know well the territory they were skirting. Often, more dire prospects are hinted at by having a bound and gagged miss reflect that "anything could happen!" Such an open-ended threat is suggested at the end of the next incident involving the abduction of Anne and Jean:

They plunged through the tree bush and then she heard the scuffle of feet on sand. They were on the beach. What was going to happen to them now?

Before her fogged mind could try and work it out she was dumped on a hard seat. The hand was removed from her mouth, but was immediately replaced by some sort of a gag. A handkerchief she thought. Then her hands were tied behind her back.

"That'll fix you," her captor said. Then addressing another man, "How's your captive, Alf?" he asked.

"A little vixen. Better give me a hand with her."

A minute or so later Anne felt something being dumped beside her, and twisting her head saw Jean being roughly gagged. And later, after they have been carried off in a boat.

He repeated the testing of the bonds and the gag, and then, with a satisfied exclamation stood up in a chair, gagged her with a sponge and a scarf, and wound a clothesline around her middle so that she could not get out of the chair.

Paddy fumed, and tried not to swallow bits of sponge as she heard the men make her beloved Silver Knight enter the horse-box. They drove off and she felt very much alone. She squirmed and twisted, trying to free herself, but the bonds were too tight.

And later, after they have been carried off in a boat:

The man bent over her, roughly tried her bonds and the gag. Satisfied they were properly fixed, he left her, and the beam of the torch shifted to her right and focused onto Jean.

Jean lay on the floor on her side.

As the man went to her, Jean straightened to a sitting position.

He repeated the testing of the bonds and the gag. "Just stay there, my dears," he said with a hoarse chuckle. "We'll be back later to take care of you and teach you not to poke your nose into things that do not concern you."

Whatever that threat involves is never discovered, for the girls are found and rescued in the nick of time.

As well as such close attention to capture and bondage in the storylines, a heroine in bondage was usually sufficient cause for an illustrator to turn her dramatic plight into a visual for the story, such as in "Mystery of the Masked Ball" where Joan discovers her friend lying bound and gagged in her harem costume, there is a fetching line-drawing that shows Joan bursting in upon the helpless Belinda, staring wide-eyed back at her above her gag.

Many of these color illustrations, it should be noted, are minor masterpieces, transforming a simple discovery like the following into a classic of bondage eroticism. Sometimes it is quite amazing how a passing reference to a girl being tied up can generate a major illustration for the story.

A humble line like - "I found Sally tied up in the attic" - from "Stella Solves a Mystery" on page 12 of Spotlight Stories for Girls, inspires the full-page color fronts-piece illustration in that storybook. Here we see the heroine, Stella, looking over the edge of a ladder to discover her missing friend sitting there in her school uniform, her wrists and ankles bound, a gag round her mouth.

Whichever way you look at it, it is a marvelous return for such a simple reference. Little wonder girls found their brothers pouring through their storybooks.

The late evening sun streamed into the room she entered. It was well enough furnished with old Victorian stuff, severe and well polished. On a horse-hair sofa lay Sydney, bond and gagged. Lu-lu acted with astonishing promptitude and presence of mind.

Lu-Lu unties her friend, but because an artist chose to bring this moment to life in a gem of bondage art, its impact has been increased a thousand- fold.

Now we see Lu-Lu entering the room, her eyes filled with surprise and wonder at what she sees before her. Sydney lies on the sofa totally in bondage, her arms, wrists and ankles bound firmly with stout rope. A white cloth gag has been tied across most of her face, showing only the girl's eyes. She is completely, unmistakeably helpless, not one of these over-resourceful heroines who can slip a rope or dislodge a gag. It is an exquisite moment.

So, never sneer at these long-ago tales. They contain bondage episodes as vivid and dynamically exciting as the more obvious sources already widely discussed. This writer, for instance, will never ever forget the edition of Peter Pan and Wendy he received as a junior art prize in 1955, and the distinctly odd and wonderful feeling he got when he read:

Wendy was the last to come out of her tree; and there were all her boys taken prisoner. Hook bowed, much too politely, and made her take his arm. Soon she, too, was tied and gagged, to the mast of the Jolly Roger.

I was a kid at the time, but without doubt that one picture is the first I remember, a vital trigger along with the phrase "tied and gagged," and so becomes a reason why I am here in this fine and unique magazine today, writing this and pondering these wondrous thoughts.

THE SCENE THAT SETTLED INTO MY SOUL AND IMPRINTED ME. THERE I WAS, THEN SUDDENLY . . . WHAM!
What triggered your interest in bondage?
(Remembrances of first impressions)

Cowboys and Indians as a child.

•

I was 10 or 11 and playing cowboys and I tied an older girl to a tree. Hot dam! Hot diggity!

•

Movie scene – "Apache"

•

I became very turned on at the age of 12, capturing a next-door neighbor girl of 13 and tying her up during a game of cowboys and Indians involving about 10 kids.

•

Movie serials of the early 40's. They were great. And comics.

•

Movies: "Ginger" and sequels. Roy Rogers and Dale Evans.

•

Mostly just fantasizing about women in bondage.

•

Photo of a girl in the "bound lotus" yoga position.

•

Cover photo and paperback detective novel about 25 years ago.

•

Watched a friend tie up his younger sister. I was 5.

•

A scene from the "Dark Shadows" soap. Victorian-dressed damsel gets bound to a chair and gagged with cloth. I was 10 or 12 years old.

•

Probably when I was a baby. I had been tied one or two times in my bed wearing knitted wool dresses.

•

Old Italian Roman Empire flicks.

•

1953 movie serials: Kay Aldridge, Adrian Booth, Linda Stirling. Lois Lane in the old Superman TV series.

•

I think it comes natural to me. At least I don't recall any particular event instilling it in me. I remember I enjoyed tying and being tied as far back as when I was 5 and 6 years old.

•

Like many people, when I was a teenager, I thought I was the only one in the world with this strange passion. Of course, when I got older and ventured into an adult bookstore, I found I was not alone. I think this is why there's an overabundance of males in the bondage community. Women don't go into adult bookstores so they aren't exposed to that whole world of bondage.

•

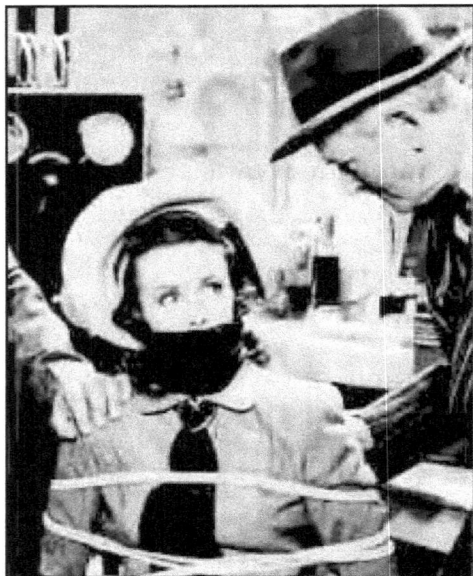

Serial imprinter Noelle Neill as Lois Lane.

Pre-teen fantasies and movie scenes.

•

A handcuffed heroine scene from the

novel "Don't Catch Me." Can't recall the name of the author.

•

I had my bondage fantasy since I was in grade school. I grew up in a small mining town, and Saturday afternoon movies were the thing to do. The Superman series was the best—almost every episode had Lois Lane tied up.

•

As far back as I can remember, I have always been interested.

•

A photo or a movie, then I roped my wife and took pix.

•

Can't say, just realized that I always get stimulated by bondage sequences on TV

•

I tied and gagged a girl in elementary school and was punished for it.

•

Tying up games as a kid always caught my attention.

•

When I was about 4 or 5, I saw an episode of "The Lawman" which had a very intense scene of Peggy Castle being bound and gagged by a bad guy. I felt the same way I did when I touched an electric fence.

•

Comic book cover at 4-years-old.

•

Watching my older sisters and girlfriends tying each other and the movie "Jamaica Inn."

•

A movie bondage scene in an old western I was very young, and the sight of the helpless heroine bound to a chair and gagged triggered feelings that were new and exciting.

•

"Diana" serial cartoon ad in one of dad's magazines

•

Probably Lois Lane in "Superman." But the interest has been there as long as I can remember.

•

Don't remember. Do remember playing cowboy and tying myself up at age 8 or 9. Switched over to cowgirls at age 12.

•

One of the earliest films I saw that got my attention was "Prince of Pirates" with Barbara Rush.

•

Pre-puberty bondage excitement when tied up by others.

•

Movies and pictures in children's books.

•

I was always fascinated seeing a female bound in the movies or on TV. The sexual connection came to me independently before I ever heard of bondage as a means of sexual expression.

•

When young, I often tried to tie my sister during play, but she never went along with it very well.

•

Games as a boy. Tying girls. Used tape to tie and gag a girl once.

•

We tied up my friend's sister once. I've never gotten over it, never forgotten how exciting it was.

•

Mrs. Peel in "The Avengers."

•

Early old movies influenced my bondage tastes a great deal. Be it mystery or comedy, there was always a pretty girl being bound and gagged at some point.

•

I was transfixed at age 5 by a "Dick Tracy" strip in which a blonde, young girl is tied and gagged to an upright backed chair. It was on the cover of the Sunday New York News comic section in full color. I have searched for years and never been able to find it again.

•

I cannot recall my age when I was conscious of the effect a bound female had on me, but I do recall a quiescent female having her wrists bound behind her.

•

I was in my teens when "At the Villa Rose" came into my hands, and since then have enjoyed many novels having bondage as themes.

•

Photographs in a man's magazine showing a model wrapped in chains. I was surprised how much impact it had on me. Cowboys and Indians as a lad. I have enjoyed seeing a girl tied and gagged since I was 10 years old.

•

A neighborhood girl, Lucille, used to let me tie her up while I folded my newspapers for deliver. It took me a long time folding those 100 papers. I would also take her for a bike ride blindfolded. She liked it and so did I. I didn't know why, but I always got thrilled and excited when I tied her. We moved away and I never saw her again. I wonder if she remembers.

•

When I was in the Navy, I saw a bondage ad and waited for the catalog to come. I was thrilled to see so many lovely girls all tied and gagged. I wish I had those catalogs today.

•

I saw a print of a beautiful girl bound and gagged.

•

I used to put myself to sleep fantasizing about girls tied up.

•

Stefanie Powers in "The Girl from U.N.C.L.E." TV series.

•

Probably watching Dale Evans and other women in western movies being grabbed, gagged and tied. Later, in playing cowboys and Indians, I would enjoy tying up girls as captured prisoners.

•

I don't really know. It must have been a photo when I was very young—3 or 4.

•

When I was bound by my aunt, who was 7 years older. I was 9. She had me standing at the foot of a four-poster bed with wrists to each post and ankles spread to each post. She refused to let me go for some time. There was no sex, no gagging, just verbal teasing.

•

Covers of detective magazines and old movie scenes.

•

Always I had these feelings about damsels in distress. Then, later, when I saw "The Collector" and Yvonne Craig in "The Man from U.N.C.L.E" and Bethel Leslie bound in a Richard Boone television show.

•

Lois Collier bound and gagged in "Jungle Queen" and Wanda McKay bound and gagged as a cowgirl in "Raiders of Ghost City."

•

I was tied up by an older girl when I was 6; I returned the favor a few days later.

•

Remember the TV series "Mod Squad?" In at least two episodes, the actress Peggy Lipton got tied up. I can recall being fascinated with her predicament.

•

A girl dressed in lingerie masturbated while bound by herself. She knew I was watching and seemed to enjoy it.

•

I can't answer that, except to quote one of Havelock Ellis's patient case studies: "It seems to me that I happened on these ideas myself and that no one suggested them to me." However, I fantasized binding neighborhood girls at the age of 6 or 7.

•

I think comic books had an effect on me. Something sexy about Wonder Woman being helpless when tied with her own lasso.

•

I have enjoyed seeing a girl tied and gagged since I was 10 years old. I don't know how it started.

• • •

THE IMPRINTERS: "AND HOW DO THE BEAUTIFULWOMEN WHO ROLE PLAY YOUR FANTASIES FEEL ABOUT IT?"

In my mind, it may have something to do with a man's power over his mate. I can see how it would be a turn-on. I have thought of handcuffing a man to a bed and just going for it. Having all that power at my fingertips would give me a sense of fabulous excitement. I can sense the thrill that would be involved.

PIA SANDS – Bondage Life 23

I think this goes back even further than puberty experience, all the way back to being at the mother's breast, being completely helpless. I could like that, but I think that as a man it may be even more pleasurable because you have to shoulder the burden of all this responsibility and have to keep a "stiff upper lip.' So I think it could be even more pleasurable for a man because he can relax completely and accept the comfort of being helpless and taken care of.

MARIA TORTUGA - Bondage Life 32.

They may have thought that bondage would be a restriction, a loss of freedom. They'll discover that it's not, it's a release. It frees me to relax and just experience. It's a release from self-consciousness, from responsibility.

KIRI KELLY – Bondage Life 31

You can tie up anyone, or I can tie you up, but that's just bondage. If the person is intelligent, it's what their mind is doing to them that is the fun part.

SIMONE DEVON – Ladies in Restraint

I'm very much an active person and I think that comes across when I'm tied up because I'm putting my all into it. So I'm even more active when I'm tied up. There's a lot of sexual appeal about it —the vulnerability, what she's wearing, what she seems to be feeling.

DEBRA LEE – An Early Bondage Life

I've noticed something very comfortable about bondage, something that can probably be traced back to childhood. There is this feeling of being gently squeezed or held, and that is a nice feeling. I read somewhere about a psychologist who believed bondage related to mother love in a couple of ways – that being tied up, gagged, blindfolded, completely helpless in other words was about as close as you could get to being back in the womb which was the most secure place any of us has ever been.

MRS PAUL RYAN - Bondage Life 2

There is something very romantic and very erotic about the bondage fantasy as far as I'm concerned. It has appealed to me since I was a child, and I always loved it when we played games and I got to be the maiden in peril. I always wanted to be the person tied up.

LAUREL BLAKE – Bondage Life 21

LAUREL BLAKE LOOKS AT LOVE AND BONDAGE...
Q: What's your take on how often lovers should make love?
A: As many times as both parties want. I don't know the number. Times change, situations change, there are times in your life when you want sex more than at other times. I think a good lover will know and understand what or when it will be good for both people and play it accordingly. At one point in your life, it might be every day, sometimes every other week. It depends on the situation, what's going on in the re-

lationship. It's got to be good for both people before it can be good at all
.

Q: How often should a good bondage partner tie you up?

A: Anytime I ask for it, or whenever he thinks it would be fun. I don't always associate bondage with sex. You can have great bondage without sex. You can have lots of fun. I think whenever the mood strikes you.

Q: What do you think about when you're tied up?

A: Mmm, when I'm tied up, I think about a lot of different things. A lot of them are very personal thoughts which I really wouldn't want to talk about. But I do sometimes think about certain men and how much I would want to tie them up and what I would do to him once I had him tied up. Sometimes I actually think about Gwendoline and I remember various scenes of her being tied up and I wonder if this is going to be like that. Lots of things go through my head and different things every time I'm tied up, different positions. I always daydream.

Q: If I suggested to you that those ropes were your lover's arms... you're lying there being squeezed, what do you feel? Not what you think, but what you feel.

A: When I'm tied up, I feel very secure. It's an almost comfortable feeling, an almost nurturing feeling. If those were my lover's arms, I would feel completely enfolded, a very warm and safe feeling.

The Bound Beauties of Harmony

Nearly a thousand lovely women posed in bondage for Harmony's audiences. Some were actresses and models. One was a best-selling author. A couple practice law. Others were business owners and some were housewives

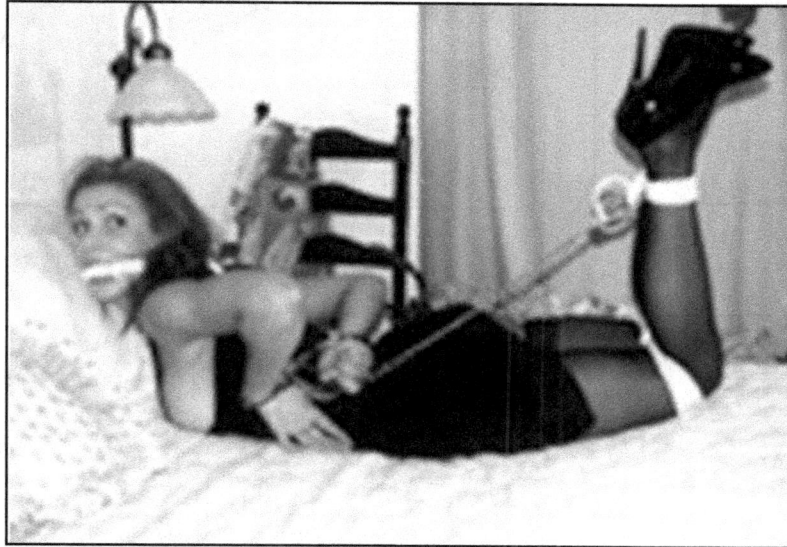

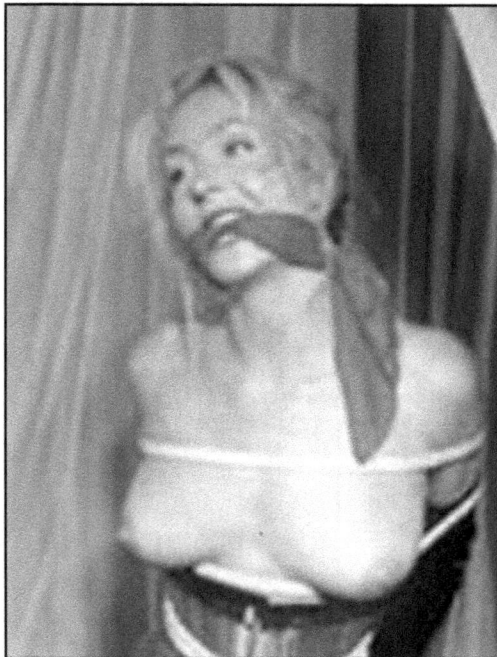

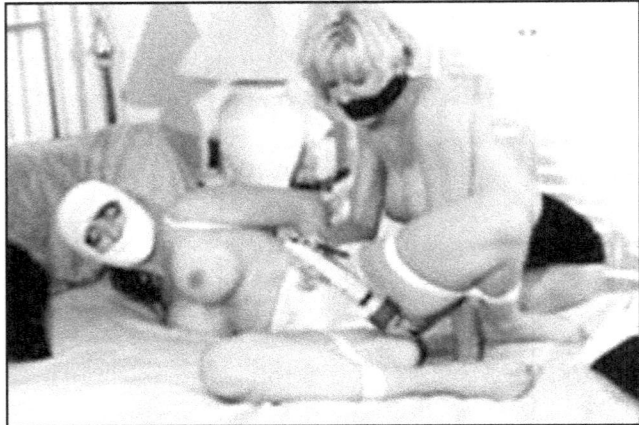

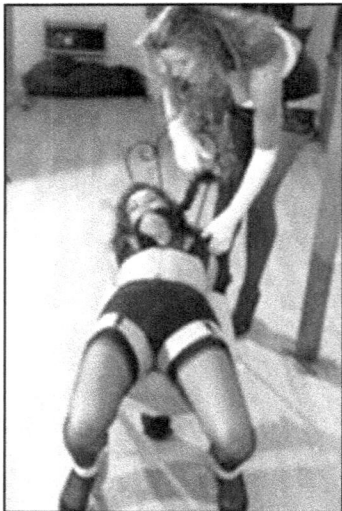

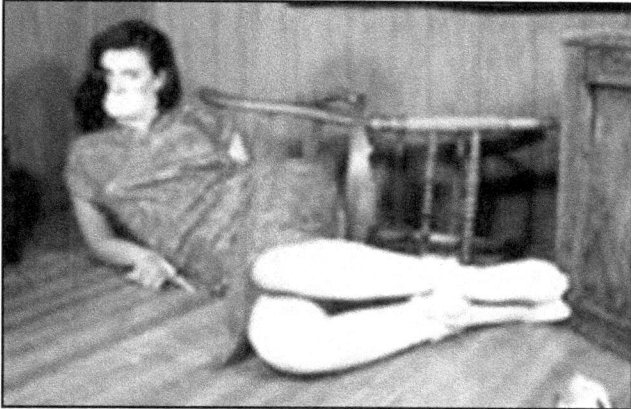

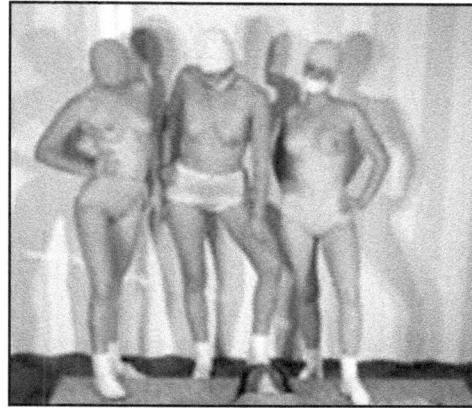

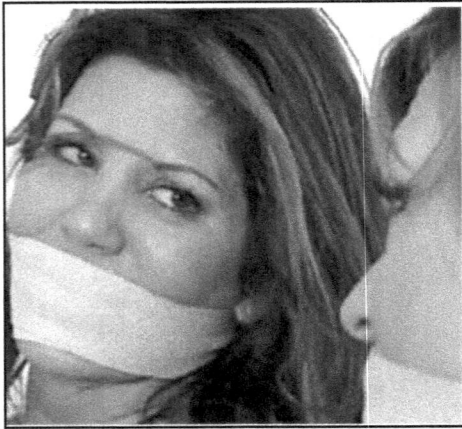

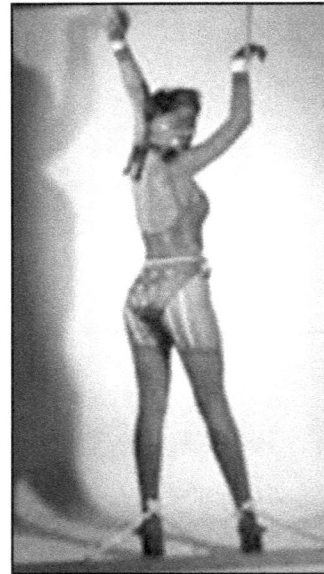

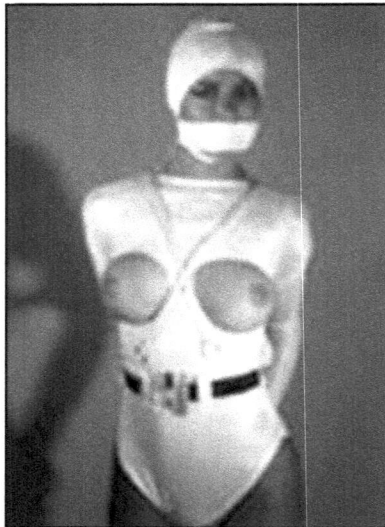

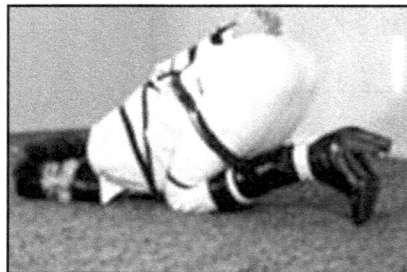

PART THREE
Bondage on-screen

BEHOLD THESE MOVIE STARS IN BONDAGE! These are samples of a "Name That Actress in Bondage" photo quiz that appeared regularly in Bondage Life. Might be that one or more of these scenes created an erotic lifelong positive bondage impression on some folks out there in the audience.

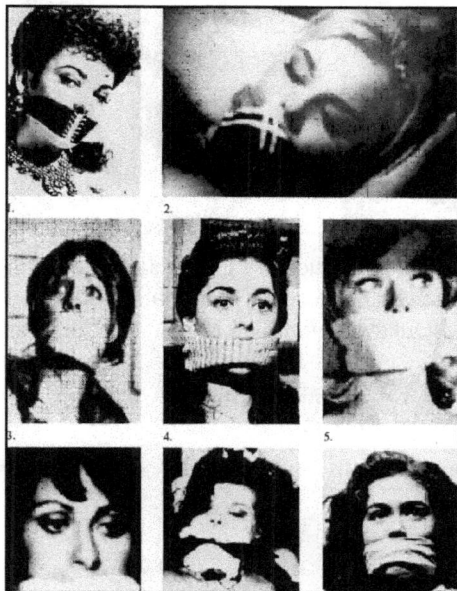

L-R, Linda Darnell, Unknown, Unknown, Unknown, Anne Francis, Elisabeth Ashley, Samantha Egger, Barbara Rush.

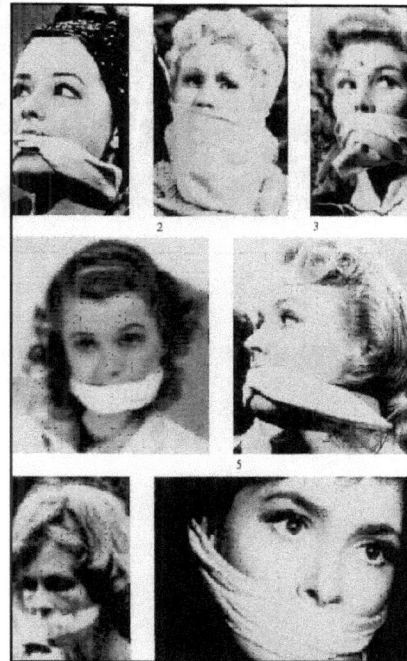

L-R, Jane Greer (Dick Tracy serial) Virginia Mayo ("King Richard and The Crusaders"), Unknown, Ellen Drew ("Buck Benny Rides Again") Anne Jeffreys (Dick Tracy serial), Unknown, Gina Lollobrigida ("Fan Fan The Tulip")

Top to bottom, left to right here are Maureen O'Hara ("Jamaica Inn"), Virginia Mayo ("The Secret Life of Walter Mitty"), Brigitte Bardot and Jean Moreau ("Viva Maria"), Dorothy Provine ("Kiss The Girls"), Jane Russell ("The Outlaw"), Veronica Lake ("This Gun for Hire"), Maureen O'Hara ("The Black Swan")

All photos courtesy Movie Star News, New York, New York

OOO LA LA -- ROPES AND 'ROMANCE

The first thing we noticed about the French film "Romance" is that it's one of the most sexually explicit movies ever to hit America's cineplexes. The next thing, even more important, is that it introduces bondage into the context of loving sex more firmly than any mainstream movie in memory.

The Los Angeles Times, warning readers of the movie's adults-only content, summarized its themes as "graphic hard-core sequences of bondage and various sexual acts." That sounds a little alarmist, but it's on the mark.

"Shall I dominate you?" Robert asks Marie. And later: "Shall I blindfold you?" The answer to both questions is a hesitant yes, and the blindfold leads to ropes and cuffs and gags and all the accoutrements of bondage. The sexually frustrated Marie, played by Caroline Ducey, is on an odyssey of discovery that has led her from one graphic physical encounter to another (including one with a character played by a prominent Italian porno actor, which gives you an idea of the kind of onscreen sex we're talking about here. The guy's a perfectly good actor, but let's face it, he wasn't hired for his acting.) None of the affairs fulfill her until she connects with Robert, an older man whose ordinary looks belie his masterful lovemaking technique. He correctly surmises that Marie needs someone to master her, to symbolically take away her freedom so that she can be stripped of all responsibility along with her clothes and give herself up completely to the experience. It's a mind-set that recalls "Story of O," and some viewers might look on it with suspicion as some kind of male fantasy.

But just like "O," "Romance" is the work of a woman— director and screenwriter Catherine Breillat. Under Mlle. Breillat's direction,

Marie and Robert act out two bondage scenarios. In her first experience at being bound, he gags her with a fetishistic over-the mouth leather strap gag with a rubber ball insert, positions her with her back against a post and ties her hands to it over her head. Her skirt is hiked up, revealing her pubic hair.

Then he awkwardly maneuvers a chair sideways between her and the post and ties her ankles apart, one to each leg. But something's amiss. Marie begins weeping. Untying her quickly, he carries her to the bed, where he strokes her and admonishes himself for being too rough.

The dominant Robert, it seems, is really a very gentle soul who can't stand the thought of really hurting anyone. It's all right, she assures him through her tears. She was not hurt, just overwhelmed by it all. He begins a complicated tie-up, binding her elbows together with several turns of rope. He attaches her ankles to the leather cuffs of a steel spreader bar....

The next time, things go better. She comes to him in a bright red dress, a symbol of her growing sexuality. In a comic scene, Robert rummages wildly through his box of goodies, extracting item after item of B&D gear. Then he starts to handcuff her right wrist to her right ankle, but changes his mind and instead cuffs her wrists together behind her back. For the final touch, he stuffs a black chiffon scarf into her willing mouth and adds its mate as a muffle-gag. Then out comes a small pair of scissors, with which he carefully cuts a slit in her panties. The next instrument he uses is his finger. This is pretty sexy stuff, the scenes charged with more eroticism than even the hard-core sequences elsewhere in the movie.

Our one quibble is with the level of Robert's on-screen ropework: it's atrocious. As opposed to that earlier Italian, this guy was definitely hired for his acting ability, not his technical expertise. He should have taken a few knot-tying lessons before filming. As it is, he'd barely make Tenderfoot rank in the Boy Scouts.

Enough quibbling, though. "Romance" pushes the envelope out to another place. After this, it may be a little more acceptable for a film to show erotic bondage as a natural expression of physical love between two adults. With a little sex thrown in too, maybe Catherine Breillat's brave movie is a small crack in the dam that has kept bondage and serious erotic films separate for too long.

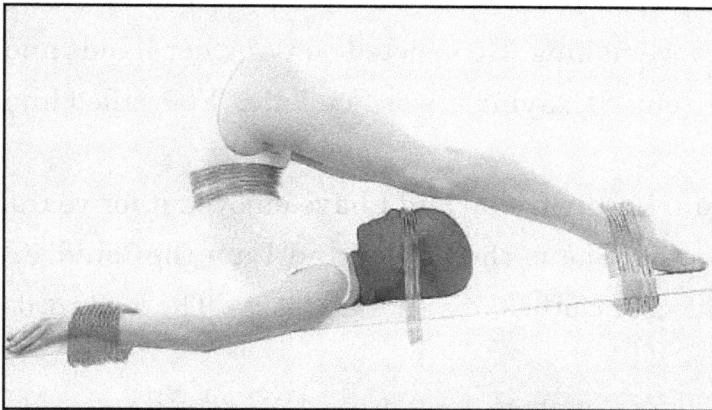

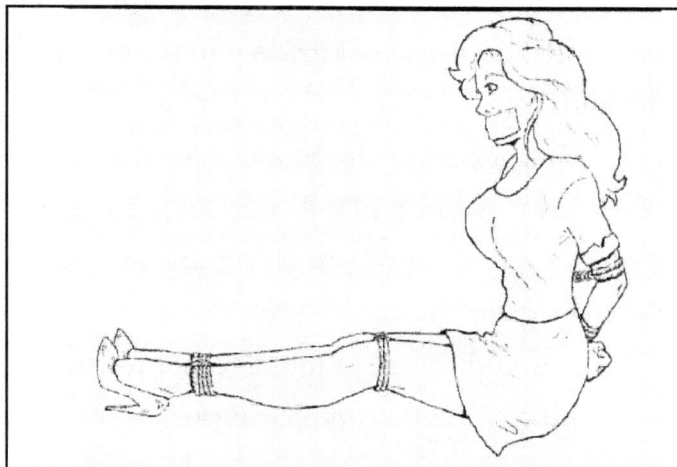

PART FOUR
Scattered thoughts from some ladies and gentlemen who actually live the bondage life...

Dear Ann Landers:

A while back, you printed a letter from a woman whose husband wanted to spice up their lovemaking. He insisted on tying her hands and feet with silk scarfs. She refused, saying it was "sadistic." You called him "kinky."

Bondage can be fun. My girlfriend and I have enjoyed it for years. Sometimes we reverse roles. She is the binder and I am the "bindee." There is no slapping, hitting or clothespins on the breasts. The key words are "mutual consent."

We play another game called "Make Believe." We take turns making up situations to act out, for example: I pick her up in a bar and pretend that she is a hooker. We play our respective roles, and it's very stimulating.

Another scenario: She is a lonely working woman who is spending yet another evening alone, wondering why romance has eluded her. An attractive man shows up to repair the furnace. Your imagination can take over from there.

Granted, these games are not for everyone, but they can enhance lovemaking to an incredible degree.

Hedonist in Woodland Hills, Calif.

Dear Woodland Hills,

The mail on that subject was mind-boggling. I had no idea so many people in the United States and Canada were tying each other up. The final word from here is — whatever turns you on is OK, so long as there is mutual consent and no inflicting of pain.

From an Ann Landers column

Dear Ann,

I was interested in the letter from Mrs. B.F., whose daughter and boyfriend played bondage games. I can see why you shied away from giving positive advice. The subject known as "Bondage' is little understood by the average person, and is complicated by its abuse by sadistic persons and by the lurid publications that focus on it.

You are right in saying that their games will lead to "kinky sex" as their relationship develops. However, my husband and I maintain that kinkiness is not necessarily bad. We feel that it makes sex more interesting in the same way that seasoning makes food more interesting. My husband likes me to wear stockings and garter belt. That would probably be defined as a fetish, and is therefore kinky. But he likes it, I enjoy him liking it, so where's the problem?

I think the two people your column was about are approaching bondage in a very good way. They are playing their bondage games openly, and unashamedly, and for their mutual enjoyment. As their friendship matures, sex is inevitably going to enter the scene anyway, and the presence of bondage won't necessarily make it any heavier than it would otherwise be.

My boyfriend introduced me to bondage when we were both 19, a year before we were married. That was years ago. At that age it was inevitable that there should be sexual overtones involved. Like your correspondent, I was fascinated by the sensation. He was skillful and gentle

79

with the cords and very attentive to me.

I loved it! Since then, it has brought us both much pleasure and has kept variety in our intimate relations. Our practice varies from Bondage-For-Fun on a Sunday afternoon to romantic evening bondages.

Just to ease the minds of the liberationists who might feel that a woman's role in bondage is one of subjugation, I will say that I probably invent as many variations to the game as my husband does.

Sincerely, Mrs. P.L

BONDAGE WAS RIGHT — THE MAN WASN'T

I met a man on a personal date line. We spoke to each other over the phone and he told me of his fantasies.

At first, I was a little scared, but he then sent me some Harmony books and videos. After looking them over, I began to get interested. I got to see a video with Darla Crane and I wasn't so afraid anymore.

Many of the magazines that he sent to me were done in the Eighties. The models then had nice expressions, that also caught my attention.

Before I met this man, I never even thought of bondage as a playful, exotic thing. I thought of it as, I'm not sure how to say it, as something hurtful. When I got the videos and watched them myself, I noticed it wasn't something to be afraid of. I was very interested by myself.

Finally, complications kept us from seeing each other so I never really got into bondage with the man.

EMANCIPATED!

Back when I was in college, the "Politically Correct" movement had just begun. I was in a psychology class called "Sexual Awareness and Exploration." At the time, I was trying to sort out all my feelings and desires about bondage.

In the open forum one day while discussing sexual practices (it was a liberal school), I brought up the subject of bondage — my first experience of "coming out." I was immediately branded a misogynist, deviant, sicko, freak, etc. by a feminist in the class. After this negative experience I came to feel more guilt and self-doubt about who l was... and the contemplation of again trying to suppress my inner desires. Later that week, I was at the adult bookstore, feeling horrible – here I was, labeled "a smutty guy" in class, and what was my first reaction? To go to a store to look at bondage books.

I bought Bondage Life 34 and when I read the editorial on page 3, It sunk in. I knew I was reading the words of a thoughtful person who had found a means of self-exploration and fulfillment and refused to bow down to the negative stereotypes other people associated with it.

Her words clarified that the woman is not a victim as some feminists insist, but a willing participant in this. It was a liberating moment for me and one in which I decided that somehow I would try to use my talents to impact the community in a positive and educational way.

I made a copy of the editorial and showed it to my professor, who read it aloud to the class. The feminist student said that this "Ki" woman was a male-dominated brainwashed pawn and challenged me to bring in the source material so she could show the class the degrading images it painted of women (she was sure that Bondage Life was hardcore).

With the gauntlet thrown down and the challenge set. I looked at my professor and he shrugged his shoulders. I said I would show it to the professor and if he felt it was suitable, he would let the class see it.

As it turned out my professor was well impressed with Bondage Life and commented that it was a sophisticated, well produced, and balanced forum for interested people, and actually a good tool for educating the public.

In class, the issue was a big hit; the professor read some "By the People" letters and showed the class the "Bound for Controversy" section with the tied-up men. The class got a big laugh although I could tell there were many who were laughing with an "ewwwww" of discomfort.

My professor concluded that bondage has been a form of foreplay that has existed for millions of years and that when practiced by two consenting partners who know what they're doing is one of the more potent forms of foreplay – much to the argument of the feminist student.

Since that time. I've been hesitant to boldly come out into the open, but at least I can discuss bondage with trusted confidants and share it with intimate friends.

Sincerely, David Esquire

I am a single, 23-year-old male and a recent university graduate, currently working as an account executive. My first experience with bondage came from looking at the covers of magazines when I was about 10 years old.

I can't remember the date or the title of the magazine that turned the switch that made me equate women with bondage, but I remember the cover. A woman with blonde hair wearing a tight black dress, black stockings and heels bound tightly with white rope and gagged between the teeth with a black cloth. For some reason that cover sealed my preferences forever. The woman was so beautiful and erotic bound and gagged. This was pretty powerful and heady stuff for a 10-year-old.

I didn't know what physical or psychological reason drew me to bondage, but I found the image of a bound woman to be pleasing. A steady diet of magazines, comic books and television shows were the fuel for my "damsel-in-distress" fantasies.

Fascinated by Bondage

Bondage is a way, albeit out of the ordinary, for a man and a woman to express their love for each other, a sensual method for lovers to let their emotions run free. Bondage is the most sensual form of sexual expression and the one that requires the greatest amount of trust between partners.

Unsigned

It's interesting to me how a woman's beauty, sensuality, and femininity are erotically and exotically enhanced when she's in bondage. I know it's difficult for a lot of people to comprehend and when I was younger I thought I should see a shrink. I couldn't understand why, as much as I was attracted to, desired, and respected women, there was this other part of me that found securely bound women erotic.

Not degrading, humiliating, or cruel bondage — I don't like that. Rather, the beautiful damsel in distress; or the lovely snooping busybody who gets caught by the bad guys, then is tightly bound and gagged, squirming, struggling, and mmmphing... All of those old and new dramatic storylines on TV series and movies that involved beautiful women in bondage. It appeals to me so much

.

Unsigned

I have been into bondage since I was in elementary school (I am 32). I could never get enough cops and robbers and all the other tie-em-up games of childhood.

Upon reaching the age where I could pursue the pure sexual excitement of bondage with willing partners, I let my fantasies run wild. Bondage is a part of my life that is always there. I enjoy it very much and I share it only with those women who have entered totally into my love life. Sex with bondage is nice, but Bondage with Love is a very special, an intimate pleasure that cannot be surpassed.

Yours truly, An Enthusiastic Reader

When he's tying me up, he gets this little glow in his eyes. Yes, I like that. I know it's old-fashioned, but I like to please him. I like him to be happy and if I can see that this is actually making him happy, I can feel a lot more comfortable with it. Obviously, the physical sensation is very pleasant.

We both have a strong interest in bondage, but with him I think it's a lot more non-sexual. It's something that's just deep seeded—a part of his being. With me though, it's a lot more sexual. Maybe that's because I was introduced to it in a sexual situation and that's how I continue to associate it.

Tied-up in Tarzana

3 Questions, 17 Answers

Q: Are you religious? Do you ever feel that your religious beliefs conflict with your feelings for bondage?

A: "I was raised with immense guilt about sexual pleasure. In more recent years, I have a better handle on my guilt, although it's not entirely mastered."

"I am very religious. I had to wrestle with guilt for a long time, until I realized that bondage was aimed at surrender and care."

Q: If you're one of the many males who enjoys being bound, what is the desired result for you? Once that result has been achieved, does the bondage still feel good to you?

A: "A closeness with your partner that's unsurpassed."

"To be in a constant state of arousal."

"Total submission in tight bondage and gag to a beautiful woman."

"Helplessness, leading to orgasm."

"The freedom to be helpless, surrendered, taken care of. Taken, bound, possessed."

"I am 'bound' by society to be in control; if I'm bound by a lover, I don't have to be in control."

Q: Why or why not do you enjoy watching a woman tie herself up?

A: "It gives me enormous sexual arousal."

"I feel she's comfortable with her feelings...I feel better."

"It's exciting to know she's tying herself for her man."

"She really likes bondage herself—she isn't just doing it for a man."

"Love. It means she loves me enough to trust me totally, and I trust her as well to treat me as I know she can."

"I love to see my partner struggle, looking at me, knowing I have control over her, but trusting that I will release her and stimulate her sexually."

"The sight of a woman in bondage is the single greatest arousal of sexual feelings for me."

"I get very sexually aroused, sensitive and loving."

"Seeing my wife bound and gagged is a sexual rush and an extreme emotional high."

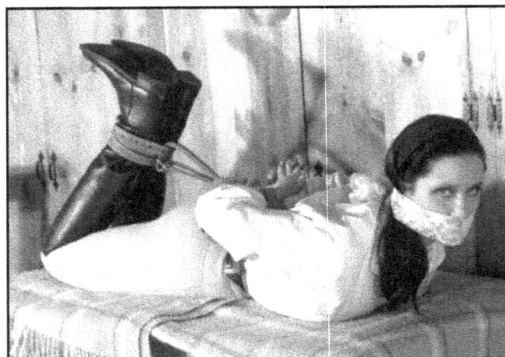

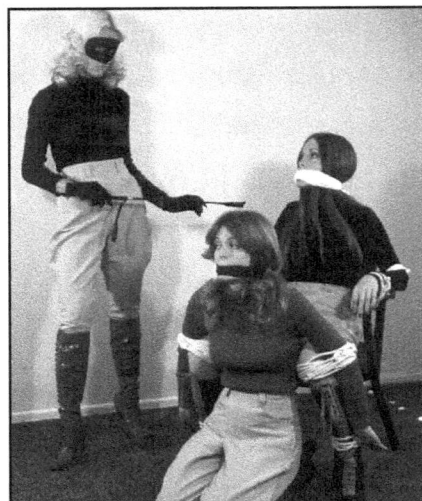

AFTER SO MANY YEARS, HIS DREAM WAS ANSWERED –
A HAPPY ENDING

It'd been a long lifetime, pretty good in all but one respect. He'd never had the emotional fulfillment of seeing in material form what he'd imagined forever in his mind.

For reasons he didn't care to explore or understand, he'd had this lifelong fantasy of beautiful women tied up—specifically in equestrienne wear. There'd been a few movie and maybe serials and some comic book scenes in the 40's, but they teased rather than satisfied.

Then, along came this expensively produced slick magazine which vowed to be all things to all bondage-interested people; it promised it would pinpoint and dramatize all the endless very specific tastes—positions, wardrobe, environment, et al. And though the magazine did in fact deliver page after page and layout after layout of beautiful women tied, it failed to nail his fantasy. As was his custom, he swallowed this latest letdown and re-accepted that it was probable that he would never see his fantasy brought to life, even on the pages of a magazine.

Finally, in one of its earliest issues, the magazine presented a lengthy layout of three beautiful women in riding clothes. Should've sizzled his soul, but instead it made him burn with resentful frustration. Because in his fantasy, the women's riding wear had to be authentic, and these good looking dum-dums were wearing high leather boots with high heels and that totally dashed whatever emotional worth those images might have had for him. Close, but no cigar. As they say, close only counts in horseshoes.

Jeez, doesn't anybody get it?!

Now he had further reinforcement that he would never ever see the scenes of his fantasies. But his subscription to the magazine was paid up and issue after issue kept showing up and he grew reluctant to even take them out of their wrappers and thumb through them. But since he didn't really have anything better to do, and even though he had long since abandoned his meager hopes, he yielded to force of habit and flipped desultorily through the pages.

Then, one afternoon, there it was again, along with the day's other mail. He opened his bills and a personal letter or two, then dragged the magazine out of its large envelope and indifferently flicked through its pages.

Until!

He thought he saw something go by that was too good to be true, so he figured it was. He decided against going back and looking for sure because he couldn't really stand up to the inevitable disappointment. So he slid it back into its wrapper and went out of his Philadelphia apartment and walked around the block.

Three times!

Now, having steeled himself, his defenses up and ready, he went back into the apartment and straight over to the table and pulled the magazine out of its manila envelope and went right to the pages that he knew would break his heart.

And there, across the two pages in full gorgeous God-granted heart-stopping soul-scorching color, were the absolute longed-for scenes of his lifelong fantasy!..a trio of blindingly beautiful women bound and gagged and dressed for horseback riding! He had trouble breathing and the room actually reeled and he swayed and staggered and fought for support to keep his feet under him.

He couldn't recall how long he stayed like that, but he remembers that he had never before known any moment of such unsullied joy. And, at that moment, it struck him that life – his life! – even as late as it now was, had at long last become worthwhile.

^

The question is often asked, "What is sensuous erotic bondage?"

Each of us has a different meaning in our minds, but we all share the basic feelings and strive for the same goal of personal satisfaction. In my own experience, I have found erotic bondage to be an equalizer. The barriers imposed by society fall. Each of us receives a certain pleasure from the experience. That pleasure is what we strive for. How we obtain the pleasure is a matter of mental and emotional struggle within ourselves.

Initially, when I was first aware of my bondage interests, I had to keep them a secret and enjoy them when I was alone. Most of us still do this. It is a natural defense. We have let society dictate what and how we should behave—both in public and in our private lives. So we carry that guilt feeling with us.

Bondage is very intellectual and creative. It also has never really been studied. I'm sure that if a serious study was carried out, we would be surprised at how commonly bondage is employed by individuals and couples alike.

Erotic bondage allows one to explore feelings and emotions safely. Take for example this common female fantasy: The woman is captured or kidnapped by one or more males and taken to some hideaway. There she is subjected to any number of sexual actions and in the end is left alone by herself. The use of erotic bondage allows the woman to carry out this fantasy without the emotional and mental strain of a real life experience.

During the bondage the experience is real. It is that loving trust between the couple that allows such an experience to be loving and memorable. Usually both partners reach new heights in sexual satisfaction through such experiences.

Jamie

Dear Harmony,

We'd been dating for a couple of months, and she already suspected that my tastes were a touch kinky because of the way I'd sometimes tied her hands together during horseplay. One evening I asked her if she would like to try something different. With a little trepidation she agreed.

As directed, she stripped down to nothing—a wonderful sight I have never ceased to adore. Very excited about my plans, I tied a scarf about her eyes for a blindfold. I told her to lay back on the bed, then I tied her wrists apart to the headboard. Her expression seemed complacent.

I then spread her legs apart and tied each ankle to the bottom of the bed. Tenderly I caressed and kissed her bound body. I paused to ask, "How do you like this?" Her reply was heart-rending. "This feels sort of degrading."

"Darling, it isn't intended to be."

I didn't release her, since she hadn't asked yet. I let my tongue wander its way between her thighs. Her nervousness about her position was transformed into sighing, moaning pleasure. I probed with my tongue and lavished her tendermost area with kisses. She was now writhing with pleasure in the confines of her bonds.

I brought her to the brink of orgasm and then entered her. She immediately exploded. Before I attained orgasm she had several more. Both of us now exhausted and placated, I untied (with a twinge of reluctance, as I have ever since) my loving lady.

That initial sexual bondage experience with Becca was incredibly potent. Needless to say Becca developed quite an affection for being bound.

Regards, Isaac W.

Hi Everybody!

Bondage has been our hobby on and off for six years now. Most of my bondage experiences have been a "spur of the moment" thing. There are a lot of times I will come home from work and get David to tie me up and gag me just so I can relax. I usually nap in bondage, much to David's amazement. He can't figure out how I relax in bondage so much.

David used to have a really hard time gagging me since I can move my jaw and pop out just about anything. I read a letter from a Bondage Lifer who suggested using a bathing cap and a lot of tape wrapped around the jaw and purchased one from the drug store. Of course, I got weird looks because I bought the cap in December.

I got home and put on the cap. Since I have a small mouth, we used half a handkerchief balled up tightly to put in my mouth. David then used three or four good long strips of colored duct tape and wound them around my head and under my chin.

This gag actually worked! I could not spit it out! I worked my jaw

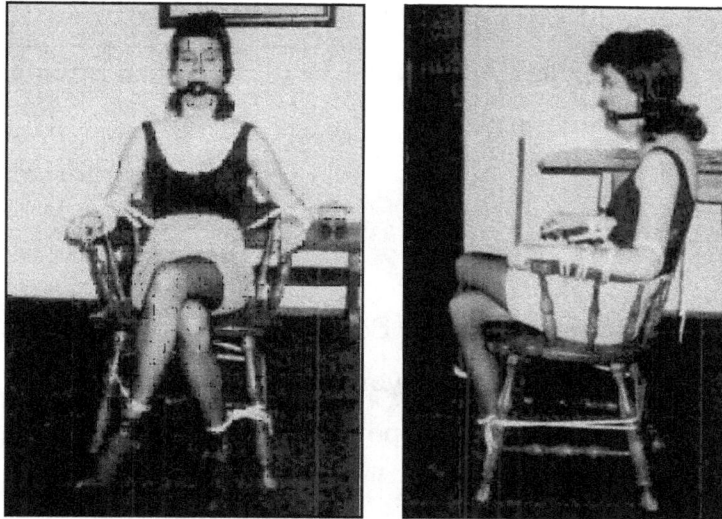

around and around until I finally gave up. I was a little nervous at first, because I realized that I had for the first time been rendered completely speechless! The fear dissipated soon thereafter, not only because of my trust in David, but also because it was very exciting. That, I would have to to say, has been one of my favorite bondage experiences to date.

Thanks for the wonderful reading material provided in your magazine. I enjoy Bondage Life every bit as much as David does, not only because I can admire and appreciate other females in bondage but because of the Harmony Philosophy. Hopefully because of your magazine, a lot of the misconceptions about bondage can be eradicated.

Happy Bondaging! Kathryn

My boyfriend has a way of getting your magazines and I think they are very interesting and we read them together. I like to read the letters from readers.

I have never been tied up. The guys around kid a lot about bondage and act like they know all about it, but I never heard about any of them doing it except one of my girlfriends. She said that a few times she let her boyfriend tie her hands behind her back and she says it is kind of a neat feeling not to be able to do anything about it when he hands get to wandering around.

Sincerely, Carol

Dear Sirs,

My wife and I have enjoyed Bondage Life since the very first issue. Since then we have collected everyone that has come out. I myself find it very enjoyable, it is honest to the point that it projects what bondage enthusiasts are really all about.

I have enjoyed bondage as long as I can remember. I introduced my wife to bondage when we were first going together. I brought it about slowly and enfranchised the trust two people had to have and the potential enjoyment that could come out of it if she kept an open and objective mind.

Needless to say we both enjoyed it tremendously. In the past four years, we have had as many sessions as frequently as possible. My wife has developed her own particular likes and dislikes pertaining to he clothing and positions and it makes it even more interesting.

Color Me Happy

The following excerpt is from the book Safe Encounters by Beverly Whipple and Gina Ogden:

"Other women prefer imaginary situations: I'm tied to a bed and he licks and sucks all over my body, tells me exactly what he's going to do, and then he does it. I am totally unable to stimulate him in any way or control his actions. I love it when he enters me, and I beg him for more. What's so exciting about this is that it's very hard for me to let go in real life, and this fantasy allows me to be out of control. I'm a bit embarrassed about the domination part. Maybe I'll get to the point where I can fantasize about controlling him — or better still, about us both having equal control."

TIE TASTING

I drove from Buffalo to B.C. I visited many cities along the way. In each center, I visited many adult bookstores in a futile search for Bondage Life. As a result of this searching trip, the following story took place:

It was a hot, sunny Saturday afternoon when I was driving through a small western city and thought that I needed a break from the Interstate. As I drove into the downtown area with the idea of getting some lunch, what should appear in the corner of my eye but a sign that said "Adult Video." All of a sudden, it was more important to cure my sexual appetite than my stomach's appetite.

I angle-parked on the deserted street, not even sure if the small store would be open on such a gorgeous day. But, of course it was open, which led to the most memorable day of my cross-country trip.

The only person in the store was the blond-haired woman standing behind the raised counter. We exchanged "Howdys" and I began to browse the magazine racks for the latest BL, which happens to be notoriously hard-to-get in my home town. Sad to say, my all-time favorite magazine was not visible.

I moved to the rear section of the store to look at the video selection and was disappointed to find an absence of any bondage related videos. So now it's either walk out of the store or possibly embarrass myself by asking the attractive blond behind the counter if she had a stash of Harmony products. Since I would probably never be in this area again, the decision was made to bare my fetish of bound females to the clerk.

When I made my (discreet?) inquiry, "Do you have any Bondage Life magazines for sale here?" her eyes opened wide, her face broke into the most wonderful smile, and she literally dashed out from behind the counter to come down the aisle to stand next to me.

At this point, I have to describe the clerk to really set the stage. She was about 25 years old, about 5'8" and 125 lbs., with wavy, blond hair worn loosely to the bottom of her shoulder blades in back and just below her breasts in front. She was wearing a white, short-sleeved blouse with a black leather vest over it. Her hips were covered with a short black leather skirt which left a lot of skin showing down to her black cowboy boots. This was one erotic-looking woman!

"I've got some of those bondage books down here," she said as she bent over beside me and pointed out ten plastic wrapped packages near our feet. It sure was hard to look where she pointed with that leather-clad bum staring up at me. My reply was a little incoherent, but she stood beside me with that beautiful smile in place as I flipped through the packages.

Not finding a BL, although there were some Harmony titles there, I turned to her and said "Is there anywhere else to look for Love Bondage books or videos?" Her reply was, 'Well, you could follow me," as she headed for the rear of the aisle. She stopped in a small alcove and pointed over her head to the video shelves. The two of us stood side-by-side looking at titles, but to no avail. "I'm sorry," she said, "but I guess I don't have much material like you're looking for."

'Well," I replied, "I'll buy some of those magazines you have up front before I leave."

She brushed by me and led me again to the front of the store. I went through the stack of clear-wrapped magazines and selected Bondage Parade 44 and Chelsea's Bondage Scrapbook 6. We moved over to the counter where I paid for the purchase. She thanked me profusely for the sale as I went to leave the store. For the entire 30-40 minutes that I had been there, I was the only customer and the telephone hadn't rung.

Since I wasn't too keen to go outside into the stifling heat, and the scenery in the store was mighty fine, to delay my departure a bit I asked her if she regularly read Harmony magazines.

"I read some of the books here, but those are already wrapped by the distributor when they get here so I really never have," she said in a demure voice.

"Have you got time now to look at these?"

"I suppose so," she replied as she looked at me with a curious smile.

She handed me the scissors that I was looking at on the sales counter and with shaking hands I cut the wrapping from the two magazines and pushed them across the counter to her. She picked up Bondage Parade, which was on top, and started flipping

"Willow"

through the pages from back-to-front in an unhurried manner.

You wouldn't believe how hard I prayed that nobody would come in to alter this scenario. I noticed her hesitate at some of the photos, especially the full-page color shot of Willow with the red ball-gag, crotch-rope, bare breasts and wrists roped behind her neck. I will point out that she looked remarkably similar to Willow, except with longer hair, and bangs down to her eyebrows.

When she got to the front page she kept her slender fingers on the cover of Tanya Fox, looked at me with those shiny blue eyes, and with a slight tremor in her voice, said quietly, "That's not bad."

"Do you want to look through Chelsea's Bondage Scrapbook?" She just nodded her head enough to start her hair moving over the front of her leather vest. Slowly this time, she looked through the magazine from front to back, reading most of the photo captions and noticeably pausing at the color pages. When she got to the end page she smiled at me again and said, "Thanks for letting me look through them."

That brought me up to bat. Not having struck out yet, I looked down at the magazines and inquired, "Have you ever played with bondage during love-making?" Since I'd never been nearly so open with a stranger before (I didn't even know her name!) this question was blurted out with no thought as to how I would handle a negative reaction.

"Noooo, but I might give it a try sometime. So when do you do this?"

"Every chance I get," I smiled. "If you are good at using your imagination, the opportunities are limitless. You can have your hands tied behind your back while you sit in the passenger seat of the car as you're being driven somewhere. You can be tied to a kitchen chair while your lover prepares dinner, or even breakfast for that matter. You can be tied to a tree, either in the backyard or out in the forest, and obviously I suppose, a bed makes a logical location for a long session of bondage foreplay. Even standing in the middle of the room with your feet, legs, wrists and arms tied can lead to some very enjoyable times!"

"You're really into this, aren't you?" she queried.

"I sure am," I replied, "and you would be too if you gave it a really good try."

"I wouldn't even know where to start."

"I'd be happy to show you."

"Right here?" She nearly shouted the question at me.

"Well," I slowly replied, "it would be a lot better if we had some privacy. Since I'm just traveling through, I could get a room and meet you there, or we could go to your house if that would be better."

"But I don't even know you!" she exclaimed.

'Well, I can fix that in a hurry. My name's Keith. What's yours?"

"Sabrina."

"I've never known a Sabrina before."

"My parents are from Sweden, but I was born in Boston."

"So how'd you end up here?"

"When I got out of college, my girlfriend and I headed West for a holiday and I really liked this city. I got a job in this store and, last March, the owner asked if I wanted to buy it from him. We agreed on a price and I just pay him so much a month until it's paid off. So far it's working out pretty well."

'Well, Sabrina, now that we know each other, shall we get together later for some examples of how much fun bondage can be? Maybe we should meet later tonight when you close the shop?"

"My roommate, Sharon, will be at the house tonight when I get off work. What am I supposed to tell her?" she asked with a quizzical look on her face.

'Well," I said, "since we're only doing a bondage seminar, sex isn't on the agenda, so why don't you invite her to be a spectator? Do you think she'll be interested?"

'Well..." Sabrina slowly said, "If she doesn't like it or feels uncomfortable she could always leave, couldn't she? Here's our address, if you want to come, be there after six o'clock when I close the store."

With that invitation, I gave her a big smile of my own and left to do some shopping. The department store was open and supplied me with four packages of 1/4" rope, two rolls of white and red duct tape and four multi- colored scarves.

The next four hours dragged by so slowly that I thought of returning to the video store just to stare at Sabrina and fantasize about the upcoming evening, but instead I just parked by the side of the road and read my latest purchases. I tried to slow my brain down enough to sort of plan how I was actually going to proceed once I got to her house.

Finally, it was six-thirty and I thought it was time to show up at the address Sabrina had given me. I rang the bell of the suburban bungalow and the door opened.

"You must be Keith," stated the pleasant black-haired woman who answered the door.

"And you must be Sharon," I replied as I looked at the roommate. She had a red and white striped tee-shirt tucked into a pair of tight, faded denim cut-offs. She was barefoot with her hair French-braided and held in place with a white elastic bow. She invited me into the living room and motioned for me to sit on the couch. As I did, she informed me that Sabrina had just gotten home and had gone straight for the shower. The sound of running water made that sort of obvious anyway.

"What do you have in the bag?" Sharon teasingly asked with a smile that was every bit as nice as Sabrina's.

"Before I tell you that, what did Sabrina tell you about me coming here tonight?" I queried.

"She phoned me right after you left the shop and said a customer had just offered to show her all about how to tie someone up so that it was fun and exciting. She asked me if I wanted to be around tonight to see how it went and keep her company. I readily admitted that I was a little curious to see what was going to happen, so here I am. I've never been tied-up, but I have had a guy hold my hands behind my back when we were making love, and I thought it would be even sexier if I kept my hands back there and he put his hands to use on other, more sensuous, areas of my body."

"If you can find some scissors, I can cut up the rope that I have in the bag. We can be ready to start when Sabrina comes out of the shower."

With that, Sharon went to the kitchen, returning shortly with the requested scissors. As she watched with total concentration, I cut the rope into ten to twenty-five foot lengths. I coiled each of the twelve cut ropes and put them beside me.

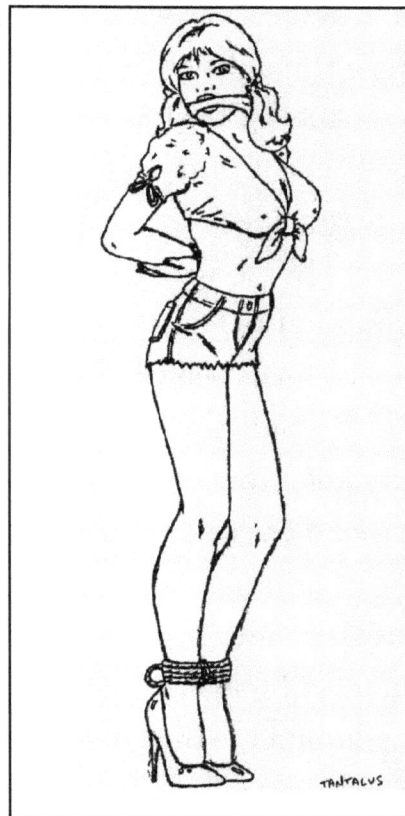

Just as I finished, Sabrina came into the room. She had changed into a print blouse and denim cut-offs, similar to Sharon's. Her wet blond hair was brushed straight back into a tight pony-tail and secured with a red elastic.

"Hi," she said.

"Hi to you too," I wittily replied.

"I see that you and Sharon have met. Is it okay if she sits in on the lesson?"

"It sure is," I replied. "She can even join in if she wants." Sharon's soft, forced laugh indicated to me that she wouldn't miss it for the world.

'Well," Sabrina said. "What are we waiting for. Let's get started."

"The first thing we should do is show you both some basic knot-tying procedures. Let's go out into the kitchen where there's better light and we'll get the show on the road." The three of us got up and I followed the ladies into the kitchen where they both stopped, turned around and looked at me.

"Sabrina, you sit on this chair and Sharon can watch over my shoulder." Sabrina obediently sat down and smiled up at me. I picked up a ten-foot length of rope, doubled it and told Sabrina to hold her hands forward, with her palms together. As she did, I looped the rope around her wrists, pulling the free ends through the loop. I pulled the loop snug and corded her wrists five times with doubled rope, then returned the rope through the original loop. Then it was two wraps as a cinch, and a reef knot on the top so that both girls could see all the details. It had only been about thirty seconds since Sabrina had sat in the chair and already she could feel what it was like to be bound.

"How about you, Sharon, do you want to stand and watch? Or do you want to feel what rope feels like too?" I asked.

"What do you think, Sabrina? Should I let Keith tie me up too?"

"Suit yourself," said Sabrina, "but it doesn't hurt at all and it's kind of strangely exciting to sit here and not be able to move my hands around anywhere I want. Sure, go for it!"

Sharon slowly extended her hands toward me, her eyes looking straight into my eyes. "We've already done hands in front so let's do hands in the back." I put my hands on her shoulders and slowly turned her around so that, when I brought her wrists behind her back, they were plainly visible to Sabrina. I then used a second piece of rope to bind

Sharon's hands, palms together, in the small of her back. At this point, I felt like I had died and gone to Heaven! Sabrina was just sitting there not moving a muscle, but Sharon was slowly flexing her fingers and shoulders to confirm that, yes, she certainly was experiencing the first throes of bondage.

"If you want to turn around now, Sharon, I'll show you how to immobilize the legs and ankles."

With that, I bound Sabrina's ankles, then her legs just above her knees. She helpfully lifted her bound wrists out of the way to make my job easier. With the end left over after, I wrapped her wrist bindings and reef knotted it to secure her hands to her knees.

"I guess getting up and running away isn't an option now, is it?" Sabrina queried. 'Why don't you tie Sharon's legs and elbows like those pictures in the magazines you showed me today?"

Sharon, who was standing in the middle of the room with her legs slightly spread to keep her balance, just nodded yes when I quietly asked her with my eyes if Sabrina's suggestion was worth following. I tied her ankles and knees in the approved Harmony manner, making it tight enough to stay there until I undid it, but loose enough that there wouldn't be any complaining for a long while yet. Then I asked her to turn her back to me so that Sabrina could watch how to tie elbows together. Sharon was quite wobbly as she shuffled to complete a full turnabout. She looked back over her shoulder to give her roommate a big smile. Then, I picked up one of the longer pieces of rope, doubled it, and looped it around her arms, just above her elbows. Then I drew her elbows together.

"Tell me if it starts to get uncomfortable," I said, and she remained quiet until her elbows were only about five inches apart. 'Well, ladies, guess what time it is now?" I teased. Sabrina said that it must be about seven in the evening, but I said that that wasn't what I really meant. What I really meant was that it was time for gags and blindfolds.

At my mention of gags Sabrina immediately said, "No, no, no!"

Sharon on the other hand remained curious and said, "What do you mean?"

I picked up the shopping bag and extracted the scarves and then helped Sharon turn around so that they were facing each other. "I put a knot in the middle of the scarf, like so, and then put the knot into your mouth. Then I tie the ends of the scarf behind your head. If you can't talk very plainly, which is very likely, just give three rapid grunts and I'll take it off you. It can't really be so bad or all those gagged movie stars wouldn't put up with it, as they often do."

They both laughed at my statement and Sharon said, "Sure, why not? Go ahead."

I stepped around behind her to give Sabrina a clear view of how the gag was installed, and then proceeded to put the knotted center of the scarf into Sharon's open, willing mouth and brought the ends over her ears. I knotted it tightly in the middle of the back of her hair so that it crushed into her black, shiny braid. As I was tightening the knot I felt her hands exploring the crotch area of my jeans, almost as if by accident, but totally hidden from the sight of her roommate.

Very slowly, I stepped back and walked around between the two well tied friends. When I asked if they were comfortable, they both nodded yes, and Sharon was actually grinning underneath her gag.

Sabrina said, "Maybe a blindfold would be okay." So I folded a scarf into a three-inch band, went behind her, and with Sharon staring intently, I lowered the blindfold over Sabrina's blue eyes. I adjusted it over the bridge of her nose and brought the ends around her head. Carefully I tucked each end over the tops of her ears and tied a square knot under her pony-tail (which was still damp from her shower, causing little water droplets to run down the ends of her stranded tresses). Then my hands brushed Sabrina's neck and throat, strictly to ensure that the blindfold was in the correct position,

I could feel her whole body involuntarily shiver.

"Now that you both know the basics of how to actually tie up your partner, how about if I untie each of you and we explore some other positions and bondage erotica?" I asked.

Since Sabrina was the only one capable of giving me an oral answer, she took her time to say that it was a good idea, but that I should untie Sharon first and by then she would feel more like getting free of her first ever bondage. Sharon just shrugged, but did her little bunny-hop turn so that I could untie her elbows and hands. The gag was the last item I removed from her because I was so pleased with the way the gag's knot interacted with her braided hair, just above the nape of her neck. When she had stretched to restore circulation she asked if she could untie Sabrina so that she could better tell how tight the knots were supposed to be.

"Sure. Why not?" I replied, so Sharon bent to her task, taking a long time to get the binding off her friend, since there was a lot more erotic touching by Sharon than was proper for an uninterested person. Sabrina, however, didn't complain at all.

From six-thirty that evening, until three-thirty in the morning, we explored as many of the variations of Love Bondage that three can do, with two-hundred feet of rope, some scarves, some leather belts of Sabrina's and a roll of plastic-wrap. But, that's another story!

Keith

Letter to My Bondage Model

Dear Sweet Marie,

On viewing latest slides of you tied up I see my own impatience to be finished with the session; for your sake, I suppose. You were well-tied-toward the end of the session. You lay belly down with your wrists tied behind with rope. Your knees and ankles were anchored to a tie which passed around your hips and between your legs (passing tightly between your sweet buns) and pulled up tight. You were totally helpless, some might say

How could you be more mine than in that inescapable helplessness? I'll tell you, Darling. Once you consent to the session, you become an instrument toward our fulfillment. I'll dress you in a black silky slip, a garter belt and dark stockings. This leaves you dressed a bit, but with your private parts uncovered.

Returning to the session above anew, we find you again lying belly-down, wrists roped behind you. Your elbows are tied, and to keep that bond from slipping you are bound around the shoulders and across the breasts to the elbow tie. Your knees are bound together, as are your ankles. Ankle and wrist ropes are anchored to ropes running around your waist and between your legs. Tightly pressing into your bum-crack and parting your labia, one on each side of your clit. These ropes pass through the rings on your bum-plug and your other plug, keeping them in place and transmitting the vibrations of your struggles to your intimate parts. To heighten your suspense, I have blindfolded you this time with a tight elastic bandage.

Your protests are stifled by several pairs of your own panties, rolled into a ball and wrapped in a long scarf. These are pushed back in your mouth by another elastic bandage. You obstinately give no sound at all, denying me the muffled moans and grunts you think I want.

You lie still and quiet, listening to the click of the camera and I touch the buzzing vibrator to your crotch ropes, you understand the position I've tricked you into. All your erotic-sensitive spots get attention at once and you can't hold back against the vibrations. Your quiet stillness explodes into bucking helpless moaning bound orgasms again and then again.

I predict that, once released, you'll lecture me angrily at first. But I know you very well; you'll find a way to offer me this opportunity again.

Love, Joe

Dear Friends,

After my first bondage experience with Jim, I knew then that I wanted more. So it became a natural thing to be included during our dates.

Before our marriage, I was the object of Jim's bondage all of the time. We were not very experienced and were using only some rope and handcuffs for our games. One evening just before Jim came over to my apartment, I decided it was time to reverse things. I knew we were both particularly horny. I was dressed in his favorite lingerie of stockings and garter belt and a slinky transparent gown.

When Jim knocked on the door, I answered the door dressed that way. To say that Jim was surprised is an understatement. I quickly pulled him inside and locked his hands behind him with the handcuffs. He started complaining that he didn't like this, but the bulge in his pants said different.

I unfastened his belt and pulled down his pants and underwear. His cock immediately jumped to attention. I began to caress his cock and balls. All of a sudden his complaining turned to moaning. He sure seemed to be enjoying it. I dropped to my knees and took his cock into my mouth.

The hardness of his cock made me drip with desire.

I pulled his pants up and led Jim upstairs to the bedroom. I forced him down on the bed and removed his clothes. I told Jim I would remove the cuffs if he would agree to let me tie him up on the bed with some rope. He was so horny he immediately agreed.

I tied his arms and legs to the bed frame. I next took off my gown and laid down next to him and pulled the covers up over us. As my hands explored every crevice of his body and I felt his hard cock, I knew that from then on we would be exchanging roles from time to time.

I climbed over Jim in position to make him lick me. This positioned me to suck his cock and balls. All of a sudden Jim had his arms free and was tying the ropes to my ankles. My first bondage job wasn't the best As we continued to play, we lost interest in the bondage and began to make love. After that hot session we were both too tired to go out on our scheduled date. We spent the rest of the evening talking about the experiences we had just had.

As the evening progressed, Jim began to get excited again. Jim wanted to show me the proper way to tie ropes so that escape was impossible. Since I was becoming excited again, I agreed to be the victim once again.

As Jim was tying me to the bed he delivered a running commentary on the bondage. His description of the bondage as he was tying me up was making me horny.

After I was securely tied, Jim demonstrated that the ropes were in fact escape-proof. He tickled me for several minutes without letup. I pulled and strained as much as I could, but I couldn't get free. I had been securely bound. I asked if he would now trade places so I could practice. He agreed and untied my arms and legs.

I positioned him on the bed and tied his legs as far apart as I could get them, keeping the knots out of reach near the bed frame. I had a neat idea. I grabbed the handcuffs and snapped them on his wrists before he knew what was happening. Then I took a piece of rope and tied his cuffed wrists to the bed frame over his head. There, that ought to hold him for a while. I had never seen his cock so hard before!

For the first time in his life, Jim was tied so that he couldn't escape. I kept him that way for the rest of the evening. I teased and tickled him without mercy. This was my first experience at having a man this helpless and boy did it ever make me happy. I must have had ten or eleven climaxes that night.

After the evening was over, we snuggled up and talked the whole thing over. We decided that while we enjoyed me in the submissive role the most, turnabout on occasion was also great fun. It was that same evening that Jim asked me to marry him. It goes without saying that I accepted.

Over the next few months we played a few games, but were mostly too busy with planning to get into anything involved. During all the planning we came to a mutual agreement that we would be married while each of us was fixed in bondage in some inconspicuous way. After all the talking and planning we decided that I would fix him up and he would fix me.

I purchased 4 small leather straps, 4 rings, and some heavy string Jim would wear the leather straps around his wrists and ankles under his clothes. The string would be tied around his cock and balls. Jim agreed to do that provided I would fix me up the way he wanted.

I couldn't wait for him to tell me. He wanted me to wear an open-bottomed corselet, seamed stockings, and no panties. Since I would be wearing a long dress he wanted me to put a rope around my waist and down between my legs. The corselet held the rope underneath very firm.

The crotch rope rubbed me and had me dripping with desire before the wedding even began. I almost had a climax as I walked down the aisle with my dad. If anyone noticed either of us being fixed up nobody mentioned it.

This episode was to lead to our current like of "public bondage." By the time we finished all of the ceremonies and got to the hotel we were both so hot we jumped into bed before we even finished undressing. I guess that about describes the whole day.

Boy that was a great climax! I still haven't let Jim climax yet. It's been three hours now and his cock is still as hard as a rock. I just forced the panties I have been wearing all day inside his mouth. The only thing Jim can move is his cock. I think I will rub his cock til he cums and then leave him in the bondage. He tells me this is very frustrating.

Yours for Bondage, Sue

MEMORIES OF THE MUPPETS

I can't really remember what sparked my interest in bondage. I have always been this way. I was always the lone Indian getting tied up by a few cowboys. While other people, especially as children, fancied themselves as heroes in fantasy, I always fantasized about being the damsel in distress.

Keep in mind that what I am describing is from a time before I even knew what sex was— I just knew this fantasy made me feel good inside. I also remember a favorite scene from one movie in particular when I was growing up. Try to control your laughter a little here — please. I always liked the scene in one of the Muppet movies where poor Kermit gets strapped in a chair for questioning. I used to just hit "rewind..."

When I was trying to get to sleep, I used to play a little game. (I've never shared this with anyone...). I would lie in my bed and pretend there was a machine watching me at all times. If I opened my eyes, one of my legs would get strapped down to the bed. Then my other leg, my arms, my head, my waist—and then I imagined the machine was threatening me with a whipping or spanking if I didn't behave myself. I always wondered why I couldn't get to sleep on those nights! Again, I didn't perceive this as a sexual fantasy; I only knew it felt good.

As I grew into adolescence, I began to repress these feelings. My family never discussed sex at all and they were very religious. As a re-action to all this repression, I got myself into a lot of trouble by dating "bad" guys. I was definitely a rebel and acted like a bad-ass most of the time. Only when I ended up marrying one of those bad guys (and getting out of it ten months later) did I finally take the time to figure myself out.

I had a wonderful friend through all this, and he is now my cur-rent husband. He has been the first person in my life who let me explore my sexuality without condescension or more forced repression. He has helped me to explore it in its entirety, and we've been having a blast the whole way through.

AS in OHIO

Dear Bondage Life:

We had decided that she would play a rich young debutante and I would be a burglar. Dressed in only her white slip, her silk panties and a necklace about her neck, she went into the bathroom to touch up her make-up. After waiting a minute, I snuck up behind her and clapped my hand over her mouth to silence her. I wrapped my other arm around her arms, holding her squirming body immobilized. Her wide eyes blinked at me in the mirror and her silk-covered behind wiggled against my crotch.

I whispered that I had come to relieve her of her jewelry. She made muffled sounds underneath my hand. I pulled my comely damsel backwards out of the bathroom and her eyes widened as she watched herself being helplessly carried away from the mirror. Her nipples were standing out prominently under the slip as she was pulled into the bedroom. I instructed her to lie face down on the carpet and released her. She obeyed, asking in mock fright what I intended to do with her.

I told her I was going to tie her up to prevent her from interfering, and also put a gag on her to keep her cries from reaching the neighbors. Removing my belt, I tied it around her elbows. It wasn't nearly tight enough to make her elbows touch, but it pulled her arms back and thrust her bosom up when I rolled her over on her back. She watched in fascination as I bound her wrists stretched away from her sides. I tied the ends of the ropes to the legs of the beds she lay between.

Having secured Deb's arms, I massaged her ankles, then stuck both hands straight up her slip. She gasped as my fingers clutched the sides of her panties and tugged them down. Her buns wiggled in excitement as the sheer material was peeled away from them to slide down her legs.

Removing the feminine underthings from the kicking ankles, I wrapped an arm around the shapely limbs, holding them tight as I slid a chair towards us. I placed her heels on the chair and straddled her raised legs. Holding one ankle to the armrest, I bound it snugly. I dismounted her legs so I could her other ankle to the opposite arm rest.

She squealed when her legs spread open. She giggled and wiggled futilely while I tied that leg, holding her legs raised and parted. She squirmed, knowing the gag was coming next. I thought her undies would do a great job of stuffing her mouth, but she had other ideas ("Not my panties! Not my panties!"), so I had to look for another gag. I found a washcloth in the bathroom and wadded it into a ball. "Say 'when,' " I said, stuffing it between her accepting lips. Her cheeks puffed out as I packed it deep into her mouth. I stopped and let her adjust to her gag for a minute. I'd assumed I'd have to tie something around her lips to hold her stuffing in place, and Debbie began trying to spit it out to prompt me to do just that.

But to our surprise, she was unable to disgorge the cloth. It packed her cheeks to the point that her active jaw and pushing tongue couldn't budge the thick material.

"Well, Miss, it doesn't look like you'll be interfering while I relieve you of your possessions," I teased her. I knelt above her head and rubbed both her nipples through the thin slip until they were really firm.

"Perhaps I should just leave you bound and gagged in your slip for the maid to find in the morning. What do you think of that?"

"Urr uhh! Oo beffuh unt!"

She tugged at her bonds indignantly, her bonds holding her right where she was. Then she looked up at me with her pretty eyes and stuffed mouth both opened wide. I knelt and kissed her soft hair, her warm forehead.

"What's that perfume?" I asked, trying not to grin. Debbie gazed up at me quizzically and tried to look around from her prone position. "It's coming from inside your slip," I told her, moving between her spread legs. She began to giggle and squeal, wriggling in her bonds as my head slowly moved inside her slip. I felt her body stiffen when my lips touched. I gently parted her plump lips and applied my tongue. Her thighs trembled around my head, but gradually relaxed. Her sharp breaths gave way to sighs and purring sounds behind her gag. I continued until her thighs clamped my head and I heard her grunting heavily in the throes of an orgasm.

I stopped to pull off my clothes, hiked her slip up about her waist, and joined my erection with her warm body. I lay atop her, kissing her panting face. She moaned and rolled her eyes. In between her love sound she tried to talk, but no words could permeate the gag stuffed in her mouth. Soon, she succumbed to another orgasm, and shortly after, I followed.

What a night, what a night! Okay, that's all.

Yours, "A"

THE HUNTER AND HIS TIGER

I knew it was you... I had seen you standing just within the thickening darkness of the door which was slightly ajar to reveal my bedroom. You stood and stared...

Dressed in black shirt, jeans and sandshoes, an illusion in the already deepening shadows.

The window overlooking a quiet bay had been thrown open. Moonlight spilt through it to spotlight a tied, gagged and helpless form of a girl. Enslaved to the bedposts by fine silver chains, she lay spread-eagled; a thin, smooth black rubber suit clinging wetly to her entire body. He had advanced, and now towered over the plunder. His hand entered the stream of moonlight to show the glittering of a stiletto knife; and with a skillful lick of the blade between his captive's thighs, the rubber parted to her hot, wet essence, glistening in its warm cream.

The eyes of the girl, highlighted by the white silk gag, asked hungrily for him. Yes, he had seen her breath quicken as her nipples rose hard against the rubber following the slitting of her suit. Teasingly he lightly ran his index finger over her, for having become hard himself he could no longer refrain from the intrusion of her body. Nor did she see his head follow his hand, but only knew of the glow that spread throughout as his moustache tickled either side of her sacred place; his tongue sucking and licking, like a hungry mate. licking me - slow at first, then faster, more insistently - I wait for you to cry out - softly.

And soon after, I long for you to tie me. This time not just to bind my wrists and ankles, and gag my mouth, but more heavily - bound so that I am totally immobile - a slave to your desires.

I think of you as you tie me - looking into my eyes with love, with desire; looking into my heart, reading the love and warmth, and the feeling of being loved totally that emanates from my center that reaches out for you, reaches out to you.

Then I see you sitting back and surveying your handiwork - the two of us sending signals with our eyes that say "love me." You, the master - in control of me; me, your captive - totally submissive, wanting you, wanting you to want me, at the "mercy" of your desires. I think maybe this time I might like a ball gag in my mouth - so that when you lean forward tenderly to kiss me, I am almost totally unable to respond in a like kiss — instead, my body moves; a small moan escapes from my throat.

Finally, you enter me - Oh Christ darling, I want you so much. Altho' it's been said before, it will bear saying again, and again -I can't tell you what it means to me when you tie me, lean forward and gag me. It is such a total feeling - I have never been so loved. Thank you. The gift you give to me is unfathomable.

From a Reader in England

The concept you described, "Balancing," makes perfect sense. I have been acquainted with several women who had to be aggressive in business to be successful — so to achieve personal balance, the submissive side of their personality sought release through romance. Bondage proved to be the "ultimate" in romantic surrender.

For me, "Balance" is having the scales tipped heavily to one side. I am aggressive in business and dominant in the bedroom. There is nothing submissive about me.

There have been many theories offered as to why a man desires to tie up his partner. Ultimately, the answers to this question are as varied and unique as the individuals.

I appreciate a bound woman for many standard reasons (she looks beautiful, desirable, etc.).

But what lies at the root of my passion? The key to my desire is my vulnerability.

We all have the need to be loved. We also have the fear of rejection. If I approach the woman of my dreams, and let her know of my affections, my feelings are at risk... I am vulnerable. If my attentions are met with rejection, my feelings are hurt.

So aside from all the standard reasons that I place my willing partner into bondage, at the root of my fetish is my fear of rejection — the need for her to balance my vulnerability with her own, achieved by having her bound and gagged. Her bound body insures that she will not run from me or push me away. The gag in her mouth insures that she will not verbally reject me.

Further analogy reveals that the ropes which bind her claim her to be "mine."

The gag is perhaps a symbol of chastity—no other lips but mine will touch hers. Her mouth is captured to await my kisses. For me, bondage is control, possession; keeping her undivided attention in order to win her affections and continually sustain them. Keeping in mind that this is a willing partner, the very act of her allowing herself (or even asking) to be tied reassures me that she understands my need to capture her.

Her submission demonstrates her love and her desire for me to be the one to benefit from the submissive side of her personality.

Aside from the enhancement that bondage offers to sexual love my past partners found my need to bind them flattering, a reassurance for them that they indeed had my affections. One lover explained it something like this: "When I feel the intensity of your arousal at having me bound, my own arousal becomes greater. With someone I love, who loves me, bondage excites me very much."

I would suspect that her feelings may reflect the feeling of many women who participate in bondage. For myself, and perhaps other dominant individuals like me, the need to tie up a woman and love her is as simple as the basic need to love and have that love returned – without fear of rejection, without vulnerability.

Jackson Marshall

From Donna in Kansas

Patty told me to shower and get ready to go out, so that when we got back from our spree, we'd be even that much more excited. So, after a quick kiss from her (Boy, can she kiss!), we got cleaned up. When I was getting dressed, she told me to wear the panties from the night before, with the little ties on the side, no bra, blue- jeans, and my sweatshirt with the sleeves cut off, rather than a regular blouse or T-shirt. She, on the other hand, dressed as if she were going to work in an office, in a suit and skirt she'd worn to work at the law firm the previous summer.

When I saw the two of us together, it looked as if I were being taken shopping by my guardian or something. I looked younger than Patty, and she looked very much in charge of the situation. On top of that, the rough interior of the sweatshirt kept teasing my nipples, while the lack of a bra made me wonder just how visible my breasts might be through the arm holes.

When we got into her car, we left my purse at home, and she buckled me into the car herself. I felt completely in her control, as we set off for downtown. Patty took me to a bookstore that had an extensive adult section.

We looked things over, but I didn't like the place too much, it was seedy looking and the men who came in looked dangerous and decrepit at the same time. Most of the "toys' were more geared to men's fantasies than women's desires; the shapes and sizes were ridiculous! But we did find a couple of things that looked promising.

One was a strap-on vibrating pad that I've since been told is called a Joni's Butterfly. Well, ours isn't, but it works on the same principle. It isn't meant to be an imitation of a man; it consists of a vibrating pad that has a contoured plug around an inch and a half high; it fits right into you and positions itself nicely against the clitoris, while providing stimulation on the outside of the pussy as well. It fits like a G-string, with a waist strap and a tiny thong that slides between the cheeks, and there is a little cord like an earphone cord that attaches to the control unit, which is about the size of a cigarette lighter, with a knob that controls the intensity of vibration. What this thing can do to a woman when an expert has the control is unbelievable!

Patty took me back to the car, then had me wait for a second while she went back in, coming out a moment later with a little bag that she wouldn't let me look into. We then went to the mall, where a little ingenuity turned up several things which looked promising—everything from a couple of dog collars, tiny padlocks and a leash, to some more scarves, some earplugs, and some matching lingerie that I wouldn't have thought to wear on a bet! A funny thing was, one thing we'd thought would be easy to get turned out to be impossible: a sleep-mask. No one carried them, anywhere we went. We were told we could try a medical supply store, but we decided to pass on that. But the mention of medical supplies did make us turn around and go back to the shelves, we'd almost forgotten Ace bandages!

By the time we got home, I was torn between feeling excited and feeling slightly ridiculous about the things we'd bought. The whole shopping spree had taken over three hours, what with trying things on and all. Patty suggested we take a nap, so we'd be fresh for the evening. I was a little put out, but she cuddled with me and told me to use my imagination, that the night would be glorious. I didn't think I'd get much sleep, but I did, and didn't wake up till almost four in the afternoon.

On Patty's instruction, I showered again, making myself squeaky clean, as she put it, and then presented myself to her in her room for inspection. She'd showered before waking me, and when I came in, I found her wearing her half of the lingerie we'd bought, a stiff white corset that really pushed her breasts up high, with a lacy matching G-string that barely covered her pubic hair.

She handed me my corset, which matched hers, but no G-string for me. Instead, she carefully fitted the vibrator pad onto me, lubricating it with just a little bit of mineral oil first (baby oil has perfumes that can irritate, mineral oil is better). She stuffed the vibrator control into the top of my corset, between my breasts, which looked much larger than usual in the shallow cups. My nipples were peeping halfway over the tops of the thing!

We put on our stockings, then we dressed rather conservatively on the outside, skirts and blouses that didn't show the wild undies we had on. Before letting me put on my skirt, Patty retrieved the control from between my breasts, coiled the little cord and wrapped a twist-tie around it, then slid the control into the top of my stocking, on the inside of my thigh. I wondered when she was going to have me turn it on, but she told me nothing. It was obvious that she had something wild planned, though.

We went out to eat, and Patty teased me that now would be a good time to turn on the vibrator pad. For a moment, I thought she was going to hold me to that, but she smiled and said, "Not quite yet, I think.' The whole meal was full of sexual tension, though, of a quality other than what I'd felt when I'd been out with various guys in the past. On a date with a man, I'd be wondering if he would have the nerve to make a move on me, and if it'd be nice enough that I'd accept. It's not quite true that a woman always knows whether or not there will be sex at the end of the evening; I've been on more than one date where a seemingly attractive guy managed to talk his way out of my pants, without his even being aware that he'd had a good chance, starting off.

But this evening with Patty was different; we both knew that she was going to take me before the night was over. But I didn't know when.

After we left the restaurant, Patty told me we were going to see a movie. It turned out that she was taking me to see "The Story of O" again, just like last night. But this night turned out to be different. We went into the theater and got good seats, and settled back. Patty kept on needling me in whispers, until the lights went down. Then she reached into her purse and got out a little box, and told me to lean forward and put my hands behind me. When I did so, something cold went around my left wrist, and clicked. A second later, the same thing happened to my right wrist, and suddenly I had both hands secured behind my back. The whole thing had taken just seconds; I don't think anyone noticed. I almost went into shock!

Patty had me lean back and get comfortable, which turned out to be quite feasible, as long as I kept my hands close together behind me and sat back on my fingers. I could feel my naked bottom through the skirt, and my breasts were sticking out in front of me like I was trying to show off my new corset. Patty whispered that I should relax and enjoy it. I was, but I was scared, too.

We watched a couple of cartoons, which is a pretty strange lead-in to a movie like that, if you think about it, and then the house lights went up again. I almost panicked, but in about half a minute, the lights went down again, and the movie started...

Donna in Kansas

NOT SO LONELY AFTER ALL!

Way back, when some of us were a lot younger, it seemed like there was no one else who got this strange positive pleasure from the sight of a female in distress.

It was the loneliest kind of secret. Then, in came Irving Klaw and those magazine ads of his promoting photo-sets of women tied up and gagged in their underwear. The ads got bigger and more frequent, suggesting that there were buyers for those photos, people who liked them. The happy conclusion to that was that there were some other people out there who got the same pleasure from seeing a pretty woman bound and gagged.

What a relief. "I'm not so different after all," was a lot easier to handle than, "Cripes, now they're going to tell my parents and everybody in school's going to think I'm weird" and all that.

We felt even less outcast when all those bondage magazines began splashing out across the countryside and Harmony and all the rest showed up a little later to make us feel positively respectable, if not exactly a global majority. We may not have had the other guys outnumbered, but at least there were more of us than one.

I've found a great way to tie my wife for lovemaking. First I tie her hands across her back. Then I gag her with a wad of cloth in her mouth and a torn strip from a sheet wrapped once or twice around her head and leave about a foot and a half of the sheet hanging down behind her.

I then lay on my back and help her mount me. Once I am inside her I pull the strand from the gag down, wrap it around her hands and tie it in place. This pulls her hands up and her head back. You can make it as stringent as you like. In this position I am able to fondle her breasts and neck while being inside her and driving both of us crazy.

Be careful not to put her in this position before she is on top of you as it is hard for her to maintain her balance (and besides, it is fun to take her by surprise).

Yours in great bondage, J. F. of Georgia

Hello,

At an impressionable age, I saw a Roy Rogers movie. In the course of this otherwise unremarkable movie, Roy was tied hand and foot, gagged and blindfolded.

Roy had been invincible, omnipotent, the symbol of an adult world which was beyond my power to manipulate. Now, he lay in the dirt, powerless. I then remember spending countless hours in my imagination tying Dale – his wife in the movie – to trees and posts and enjoying the fact that when she was tied, she was no longer an overwhelming, omnipotent adult.

Sexual knowledge came to me late. I had to find out the facts of life myself. I did not know what adults normally did until perhaps age 16. By that time, my sexual orientation was pretty well formed: sex was when you masturbated and imagined a tied-up woman.

Now you have this true tale of the growth of a natural sexual urge with no prescribed outlet. There is this unfocused libido in need of some nucleus.

In the theory of developmental stages, there is an age range during which sexual orientation is fixed. If, during that period, there is some sexual stimulation by a bondage scene, perhaps that nudges the person permanently. If that bondage scene is the peak experience happening in that developmental period, then, a bondager is born.

Jack in Illinois

Dear Whoever You Are:

I'm a male in my mid-30's. For three years now, I have been living with Susan, who's in her late 20s. She is, in my opinion, a very attractive blonde.

When I met her she was employed as a manager in a fashion boutique. We'd both had previous relationships which didn't last. When we met, neither of us was actually looking for a new steady relationship. However, things worked out and we became lovers. She regularly came over to my place and spent the night. One day I noticed she was in a mood for fun and love play. I took her in my arms and whispered,

"What would you say if I tied you to my bed and made love to you for a couple of hours?"

Her lips kissed against my neck as she said softly, "That would be great." As I tied her naked and spread-eagled to my bed, she kept laughing and giggling, telling me she didn't know I was so kinky. Things worked out great that time, but I felt it was too early to inform her about my desires for bondage.

On Valentine's Day, I planned a very romantic evening with champagne, candlelight, soft music, et. On special occasions we usually exchanged gifts and this time we'd agreed to give sexy underwear that we'd like to see on each other.

I spent a fortune on a garter belt, matching push-up bra and panties, long black opera gloves, dark-seamed nylon stockings and black high-heeled pumps. To complete my package, I included a pair of Smith and Wesson handcuffs.

When it came time to open our packages, I was very, very excited. It was difficult to act happy about the boxer shorts she gave me, because at the time I was only interested in how she would react to my gift. Anyway, she was breath-taken with the outfit, and when she found the handcuffs at the bottom of the box, she laughed heartily and said in a tone as if scolding a little boy, "So you are kinky, aren't you!"

We kissed a little and then decided it was time for romance. Susan would put on my gift in the bedroom, while I would change in the living room. From the moment she gathered up her things from the couch, my heart started pounding twice as fast. It seemed like hours before I heard the clicking sound of her high heels. But she was worth every second of waiting.

She walked in elegantly on her high heels, her beautiful legs exposed. Her breasts were accentuated by her push-up bra and the fact that her wrists were cuffed behind her back. She posed as a model, showing left, right and back of her figure. I couldn't get my eyes off her gloved wrists, held together behind her back. She'd actually taken all the slack out of the cuffs. Later, when I asked her why she'd cuffed her wrists behind her back, she replied that it seemed like it was proper since she felt that the purpose of handcuffs was to get her arms out of the way.

I complimented her looks and admired her form until she said "Do I have to keep standing here or have you something in mind?" She obviously was pleased with the impact she had on me. I guided her to the couch and she sat down, legs close together. I just kneeled at her feet, took the three-foot nylon rope I'd put in my pocket, lashed it around her ankles and cinched it tight in the middle. She didn't say anything, just tested the bindings by showing her ankles, then looked at me as I sat close to her. Her eyes comforted me and when she said "Looks like I'm going to play a passive role tonight," I could only kiss her and caress her body. She only had to sit back and enjoy.

Later that evening we shared our orgasms with me seated on the couch and Susan on top of me, her wrists still cuffed behind her back. Afterward, we discussed the whole thing and I admitted my desire for bondage. She said we definitely had to do it again sometime.

And we did. In the following months I introduced her to my world of bondage. I showed her copies of Bondage Life; let her try out rope, gags, blindfolds. I even took her to an adult store where she giggled like a schoolgirl while choosing a ball-gag. When she told me she was turned on by the fact that the saleswoman probably knew she would wear that ball-gag, I realized things had worked out even better than I'd hoped for.

Susan soon found out, as much to my pleasure as hers, that she could climax simply by being played with, while bound, gagged and blind-folded. She moved in with me soon after, and the past three years have been the most wonderful years of my life so far.

Yours, N.D.R in Belgium

PLAYING IN QUEBEC

I like strict bondage, tight ropes and a body that looks very well mastered.

I really like when my boyfriend takes his time to tie me very well. He places the rope at the right positions, makes sure they will not slip or get loose. I like when he adds lengths and lengths of good solid ropes to master my body and makes it totally unable to escape. Then, when I am totally at his mercy, he just plays with my body until I collapse in exhaustion.

For me, this is the best sex, just amazing.

So, I like to see women tied up as well as I am sometimes, because it triggers in me the desire to have more.

Many thanks, M.P., Quebec, Canada

Dear Editor,

My husband brought home a copy of your very fascinating magazine "Bondage Life" and I am delighted to find out that we are not the only ones in the world who do tying-up. He suggested that I should write to your "By The People" department and tell you about us.

In your magazine there is one brief mention about using bondage in achieving relaxation. I wish I could have seen the article that was referred to, because that is where we seem to fit in. I am twenty-nine years old and married to an architect. We have a lovely old house which I enjoy maintaining and my husband works upstairs in his studio.

When I was a little girl I had a fascination about being tied up, and it was always a part of my fantasies during my teens. When we were first married I told my husband about it. Up to that time I had never actually been tied. Just for fun he tied me to a chair one day for several hours and I really enjoyed the sensation. We did it again a few more times and before long a pattern was set which we still follow.

Every week I get my housework caught up by Tuesday evening, and Wednesday is my tie-up day. After breakfast my husband ties me very rigidly to a special chair, usually in our side porch which we had glassed in to make sort of a greenhouse. The chair has a padded seat and a head-rest that I can lay my head back against. My legs are tied together and fastened to the front rungs of the chair, my body is tied to the chair back, and my arms are tied together behind the chair back. We use a thin nylon cord which is soft but very strong. Then I get a narrow black blindfold which I made myself and which is very effective. Mostly I just have on panties, and gloves to protect my wrists from the cords, and my husband likes me to wear high heels.

My husband then goes upstairs and works in his studio. (We tried having me tied in the studio but he says I am too much of a distraction and it gets awkward when he has to have a client in.)

After he goes, I relax and before long I get a lovely feeling of peace and security and well-being. I can smell the fresh fragrance of my favorite plants, and I can hear the children playing outside (I can tell them all by the sound of their voices), and I can hear the mailman and the milkman come, and I can hear my husband moving around upstairs, and I can tell what is going on in the neighborhood just by the sounds. It is a wonderful peaceful feeling.

After an hour or so I get a feeling of being completely removed from things, almost as if I were seeing a bare woman tied to a chair from a distance, and I can contemplate everything about her just as though she were someone else. And I am always glad that she and I are the same person.

About once an hour my husband comes down to check on me and I get a kiss and a little touch on my front, and then he goes back to work. In the middle of the morning and afternoon he brings me a small cup of coffee and feeds it to me. At noon I am untied and I fix us lunch and at one I am tied again. In the late afternoon I generally lay my head back and nap for a while.

At five my husband comes down and sits with me awhile and we talk and have our Manhattans, which he has to feed me. I enjoy sitting there knowing that he is looking at all of me, although I can't see him doing it. When he finally unties me it always takes me a little while to come back into the world. Then I dress and we go out to dinner.

The next day I feel so relaxed and refreshed. We have talked a lot about this. We both like it and we thought we were the only ones in the world who did anything like this, but your magazine has changed our thoughts on that.

We have been curious about the underlying reasons that motivate us in this. My husband thinks it is basically a sexual thing but I am not so sure. It is true that I get a quiet thrill out of being nearly naked when I am tied, and I guess that is sexual.

The first year or so that I got tied I was always dressed and I got exactly the same pleasant mental state that I get now and at that time I never considered the tying part of it to be sexual. It was just a way to thoroughly separate me from my normal activities. The undressing started one hot day when I was uncomfortably warm in the morning and my husband suggested that I take off some of my things before he tied me up for the afternoon. I peeled down to my panties and bra and was pretty self-conscious about it at first, sitting behind all that glass, but I knew that no one could see me unless they came into our garden, so I got over it before long. Somewhere along the line my bra got eliminated and I don't even recall how that got started. Since then I have enjoyed my state of undress, especially when my husband tells me I look cute all trussed up and bare.

I have heard the word "bondage" used and never was quite sure what it meant. Your magazine cleared that up for me. I'll bet I spend as much time as anybody tied up, but we don't consider it "bondage." It is a very voluntary thing we do between us with great affection.

It is a strange feeling for me to write this letter. As of this moment only two people know about my Wednesdays. If you decide to print this letter thousands of people will know about it. Even though I don't know who they are. and hopefully they don't know who I am, it is interesting to know that we belong to a much bigger club that we thought.

Sincerely, Wednesday Bound

Dear Fellow Bondagers:

An issue of Good Housekeeping had a bondage article a few years ago. It was about a housewife who was bound on her bed with her panty hose and I believe also gagged with panty hose by a burglar. She had her legs drawn up to her wrists with a chair put over her legs so she couldn't get it off without hurting. But she got out and called the police, so the story had a good ending.

I am a 22-year-old-girl – even I know I'm quite pretty. I keep my body in good form, have long brown hair and I love being a girl and showing it. Just now I'm wearing a very tight red dress with a side slit halfway up the leg. Under that I'm wearing a very lacy and sexy bra with matching pink bikini panties and bright blue garter belt- standard not the French style – hose and of course high heels. This was the same thing I was wearing when the following took place.

I always asked our neighbor – a man – to check my place when I went away for a weekend. Every time I came back, it seemed my lingerie was different, my panties especially seemed to always be out of place.

So I decided to find out. I pretended to go away, asked this man to watch my place and then I sneaked back after dark. Sure enough, he came in soon after I hid and started to undress as soon as he closed my door. By the time he reached my bedroom, he only had on shoes, socks and shorts and he quickly removed those.

He put on a bra, stuffing it with my panties, then put on panties which didn't begin to cover him, a garter belt and even a skirt and blouse. Then he sat on my bed and did you know what while he looked at my picture.

I opened my dress and messed my hair and had a can of mace in my hand when I stepped out and told him not to move or I'd yell "Rape!" Was he ever surprised and he couldn't even cover himself in my brief attire for even the skirt was pulled up so he could touch himself.

I told him to lay face down on the floor and I tied his hands with clothesline very securely. Then I bound his ankles and just above the knees. I cinched all the ropes holding him and then I drew his elbows together and bound his arms to his chest just above his "breasts" and also below. He could hardly move a muscle! As I was doing this, his skirt moved up revealing the nylon tops and garters. Now I know why men find this so attractive. Of course, I was showing a lot too! My dress showed the crotch of my panties.

I took off my panties, turning them inside out so the part of the crotch closest to me would be on the outside and stuffed them into his mouth. This he really tried to fight, but had to accept. I then used one of my nylons to keep this all in place.

I went to my lingerie drawer, laid all my panties out and got out a vibrator and walked over to him. I then pulled down his panties and rolled him over on his belly and with one hand under him pushed the vi-

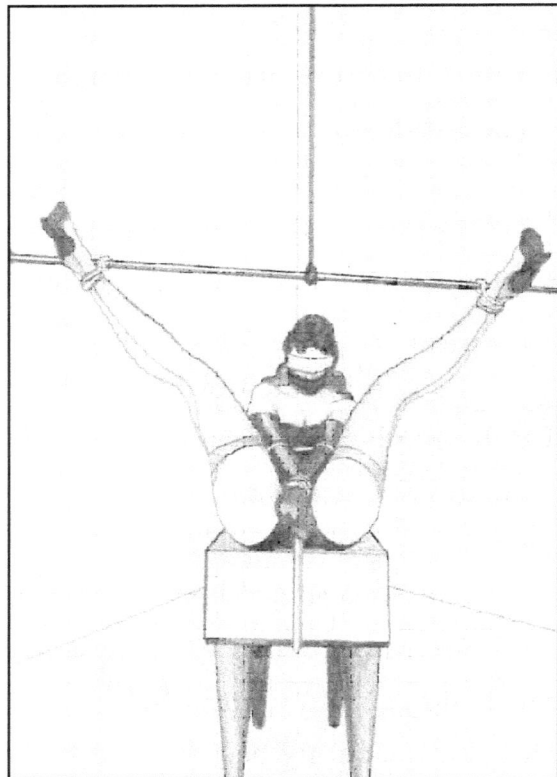

brator slowly but surely into him.

Then I took a dildo – very long and thick – and removed his gag, except for my panties and told him to firmly hold the dildo in his teeth. I then lowered myself right onto it, right over his face and then replaced all the packing back into his mouth. He must have been terribly uncomfortable with a vibrator up his rear, laying on it and me pushing down onto a dildo in his mouth, all the while still having my panties in his mouth.

Eventually, I went down on him and brought him off with my hand. Then I made him tell me in detail all he ever did in my place while I tape recorded it. I also took photos of him.

I let him go toward morning, but I told him I expected him to check my place later in the day and to expect more of the same. He came over and got more. I told him he would also have to tie me up, but that's another story.

Debra K. Pennsylvania (Note: For those who are thinking this is wishful male thinking, the handwriting on this one was definitely feminine.)

Dear People,

Several years ago, I had taken a new job with a large bank. They had a two-week training program in a southeastern city. This particular session had 11 women and two men. We spent a lot of time together and some of us got quite familiar.

One particular lady and I got very close and spent our evenings together studying for the next day. She was quite attractive, pretty face, dark hair, great figure and a deep husky voice that was so sexy! By the middle of the first week, we had become intimate.

We both had roommates so we had to limit ourselves to time alone in the hotel hospitality room. One evening, very late, I took my belt and tied her hands behind her. She didn't protest and admitted she'd been tied to a bed a few times!

Over the weekend, we had no classes and much free time. Friday night was spent with the rest of the group drinking and dancing until late. Early Saturday, I made a trip to the local K-Mart and bought 100 feet of rope, some electrical tape, three scarves and some medical tape. Then I went to a motel in a different part of town and rented a room.

I cut the rope into various lengths and taped the ends and left my bag of goodies in the nightstand drawer. After lunch, Christine and I went for a ride. When I showed her the room key she was delighted.

Once in the room, she stripped to her underwear. I showed her my bag of tricks. Neither of us had experienced bondage for a long period of time.

I chose a medium length of rope and pulled her hands behind her. After tying her wrists, I asked her to free herself. I was pleased when she couldn't. Next I selected a gag. She had never been gagged, so I just started with a scarf over her mouth. Not truly effective, But I observed her examining herself in the mirror. I had her lie on the bed where I tied her ankles and knees. By now, I was so excited I could barely stand it. I unhooked her bra and started the lovemaking process and soon her feet were untied and we were in the heat of passion.

When the passion finally subsided, I untied her and we discussed bondage. She told me it felt great and wanted to experiment some more. That was all right with me, so after she rested we got started again. This time I tied her wrists with a longer rope, behind her as before but then I pulled the ends of the rope between her legs so it rubbed her crotch. I looped the rope behind and then again in front of her where I tied it off.

Her hands were lashed to her body and if she pulled, she rubbed her crotch. I then tied her elbows to her back by winding the rope below her breasts. She couldn't move her arms more than an inch or so. I asked if she was okay and she said it felt great. I told her if she had anything to say to get it out now. When she went to speak, I placed one of the scarves in her mouth and quickly tied it in place with another. I then taped her lips with the medical tape. She didn't mind at all! I again had her lie on the bed and bound her ankles using much more rope than before. I also tied her legs both above and below the knees. Finally, I placed her in a loose hogtie.

I gave her about 10 minutes to free herself. She struggled and rolled and her sexy voice came out as a low moan. Then I told her to settle down and enjoy the afternoon. We watched TV until dinnertime.

Christine and I experienced many more bondage session and even rented the room for an additional night. My only regret is that I had no cameras to record the occasions. Next time, I'll darn sure have a camera.

Sincerely, Sam in Dayton

Dear Harmony,

I am writing to tell you about my fantasy come true. I grew up with a love of bondage but not knowing if anybody else did too. All through high school and college, I dated many different women but never expressed my desire to tie them up. I did picture all of them bound and gagged whenever I made love to them.

After college, I dated around, never with anyone for very long and never getting serious because something was always missing. That something was bondage. I started buying your magazines and was comforted by the fact other people felt the way I did. I was dating a cute girl I met at a local diner. She was a student at the local university working part time as a waitress. One evening we were at my apartment and I had inadvertently left a copy of Bondage Life out on the nightstand in my bedroom.

Well, she found it and we started a discussion on the subject of bondage.

She had some experience with a previous boyfriend. He had bound her with chains and gotten a little rough. We talked about "Love Bondage" and the importance of a trusting relationship. She said she did trust me and consented to being tied that evening. Although her previous experience was negative, she had enjoyed bondage itself. I was jumping for joy inside. I couldn't wait to finally tie up someone I cared for. We went together to a nearby store and purchased the necessary items.

We started slowly in the bedroom, with each of us taking our clothes off. I tied her hands behind her and we settled on the bed. I could tell she was as excited as I was, and within minutes we consummated our first act of Love Bondage. We agreed it was incredible. She didn't want to be untied and in fact asked that rope be added.

We then went into the living room where I bound her further. I told her to stop me if it got to be too much for her. She never did. When I was done, she was bound arms behind her with her elbows together. I had tied her above and below the knees and at the ankles. A loose rope ran from her wrists to her ankles. She struggled at my request and put on quite a show but couldn't escape. There was only one thing missing – the gag. I felt no lady is a complete captive without one. I asked her if she minded. She said she had never been gagged but if it felt as good as the ropes, go ahead. I happened to have an Ace bandage and a soft cloth. I cut the bandage I half and then placed the cloth gently into her mouth. I wrapped the bandage firmly around her mouth and tied it behind her head. This was now my fantasy come true. I had completely bound and gagged a beautiful naked woman. And she enjoyed it also!

We must have had sex six times by morning. Neither of us got any sleep and she remained bound and gagged in various positions throughout the night.

That was a year and a half ago. We will be married in three weeks. While we eventually found many common interests, we credit "Love Bondage" as the thing that started it all, and we want to thank people like you for opening the door to our relationship.

Sincerely, Dave and Lynn

Dear Ladies and Gentlemen,

My name is Carol and my husband and I practice bondage at least twice a week – usually on one night he will let me put him into bondage. I've been into it since my teens.

My husband enjoys sexy lingerie the most when he ties me up And we almost always use rope. He will gag me with anything handy. I guess everyone my age came thru the western series with the heroine getting bound. This was my experience. I had a brother a year old and another a year younger. Of course they had their friends and I had my girlfriends and would play cowboys and cowgirls. I never had any western clothes, but I hardly ever wore slacks in those days. I did have one or two garter belts and nylons.

On this one occasion, my older brother was the "bad" guy and he caught me and my girlfriend and he very carefully tied our hands behind our backs and wrapped ropes around my chest and waist to pin my arms. He then bound my ankles and my knees. As he was doing the same to my friend, her "good" guy came and tried to save us but my brother overpowered him and bound his arms and hands behind his back.

My brother then decided that he could get inside the "good" guy's camp if he wore this guy's clothes since he did resemble him. So he proceeded to take off his pants and untied his hands so he could get his shirt off. He promptly retied his hands, but laid him against me - face to face!

I think my brother knew about sex, but my girlfriend and I just barely talked about it. Girls in those days weren't as aware of sex. We knew about it, but only thought that boys got any thrill out of it. Now, the guy was 13 and he definitely must have been aware of the situation! I was forced tight against him as my brother wrapped ropes around our chest and waist. Remember, this guy is in his T-shirt and shorts - which were bulging!

Now I had never seen an erection before, much less felt one. I had on a skirt and my usual garter and panties. I had just started to wear nylon panties which were thinner than cotton. Anyway, my brother ran some rope between my legs and then bound my legs to him. He also bound our knees together. I was frightened as I was never bound to anyone before. In fact, our faces were so close together that we were kissing—just talking about how we'd get loose.

My brother didn't like us talking, so he gagged us. We were in our house, so he went to my bedroom and brought out my panties and put two pairs in each of our mouths and then used a nylon to hold them in place.

As we tried to get loose, my skirt rode up quite far - in fact, all the way up and I could feel him bulging. What I didn't realize was this was planned and we were bound so we wouldn't get loose and really – this guy wasn't even trying—he was just pumping and rubbing. I was the only one trying to get loose, but I was really participating without knowing it.

All the "cowboys & cowgirls" were now watching as this was a "first" experience for all. I found out it was also the first for my brother. We were really in a sweat and all of a sudden I felt "something" (his erection I now know) heave and pulse and we were suddenly exhausted. That was my first "orgasm" - and his! We both had our first in severe bondage and it was great. We were released - a little embarrassed, but that guy later became my husband, believe it or not. Bondage brought us together and kept us together.

I did get even with my brother, having bound him and one of his girl-friends later on. I made him watch as I stuck a couple of vibrators you-know-where. He was so erect that he came without any assistance and there his girlfriend sat in ropes twisting as the vibrator brought her off and he couldn't stop coming since he was bound to her.   Enough— as you see, I really enjoy bondage—all forms.

A Reader in Pennsylvania

Dear Harmony,

Have I ever tried to explain Love Bondage to a non-bondager? The answer is yes. Responses were varied, each according to her own experiences or non-experiences. Most readily understood the philosophy of Love Bondage, having had fantasies along those lines since girlhood. Others who had no previous fantasies of bondage listened with open minds, and whether deciding it was for them or not, understood, and did not condemn the philosophy.

From so many past encounters too numerous to mention, I honestly feel that there IS something within every woman worth her estrogen that responds to Love Bondage. Call it "Chemical," call it "Nature," but surrender is inherent in females. There are those who choose to ignore that it is a legitimate part of themselves vs. it just doesn't fit into their life and that is certainly anyone's right and privilege and must be respected.

If I tried to explain Love Bondage to a non-bondager with only a few sentences, I would say that Love Bondage is the most intimate expression of love and trust between mutually consenting lovers—the ultimate fantasy, the ultimate gift of surrender.

I would use my own lover's diary: "He has bound me and loved me, I trust him completely—the adoration in his eyes, and my captivity has become my freedom."

I wish we could all be more open about bondage. It would be nice if bondage was completely accepted, but there is a certain delicious wickedness in enjoying something in "secret." I concede that society is giving definite positive messages about bondage but these messages are still guarded. Society in general appears to want to be more open with acceptance, but is still hampered by "What would the neighbors think if they knew?"

Is bondage sadomasochism? I don't know. Do you bind your lover intending to hurt her? That is plainly sadistic. Does she ask to be bound and soon humiliated? Maybe that's masochistic.

Bondage is like anything else—it is exactly what you choose it to make it. So what if a lady is masochistic—do we consider her a freak because of this part of her personality? If her lover allows her the pleasure of what she desires, keeping the rules of safety in mind and if administered with love and trust, there is no problem. In fact, to deny her this pleasure would, I think, be sadistic.

Thanks for the forum. J.R., St. Louis

This one's from "J" in the Midwest

We feel you can get plenty of physical satisfaction with bondage and sexual teasing using good handwork and vibrators without getting into, as they said in the '90s, a "fluid exchange" sexual contact. It was good when Veronica and I actually had intercourse or did oral things with each other. With each of us making sure the bondage games ended

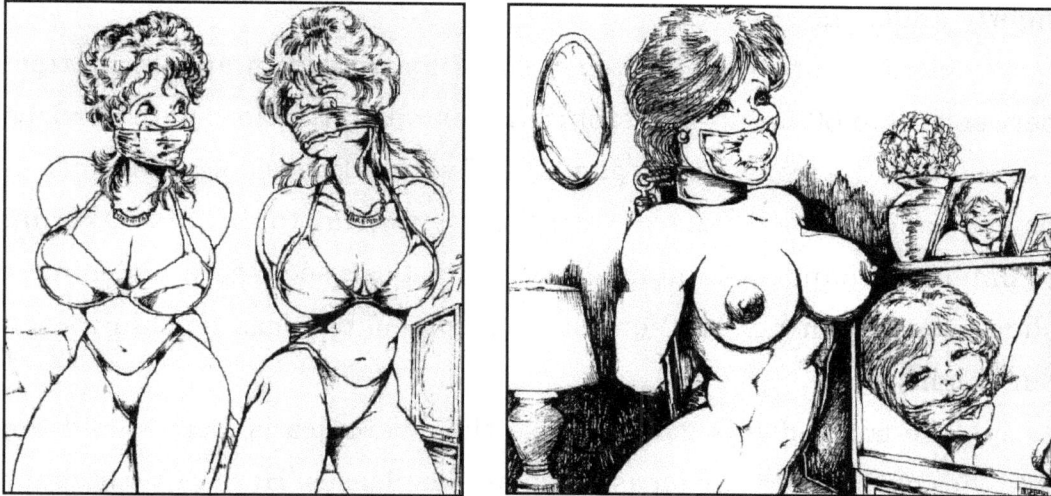

in mutual satisfaction, there was just no need to rush into the more traditional sexual acts.

Speaking of vibrators, Veronica prefers the soft rubber vaginal and to a lesser degree, anal insertion types. Since I like the feel of the female touch best, the Swedish hand-mounted type is my preference. We've got one game we play where we use a little self-bondage and autoerotic stimulation. I've extended the on-off switch on one of the vaginal and one of the anal vibrators using wires about three feet long, with switches at the end of the wires from each vibrator.

First, we lube up Veronica's orifices, inserting the vibrators. Next she pulls on a pair of panties to keep the vibrators in place. The switches are placed in Veronica's hands. You see, she is in control of her own stimulation. Meanwhile, I strip down to my birthday suit. I tie her feet together with scarves at the knees and ankles. Next she does the same thing to me. Her hands are then bound in front at the wrists using a quick release knot, leaving them semi-free as our safety out. This would allow Veronica to pull off her blindfold and gag, loosening the quick release knot with her teeth in the event of an emergency. She is then blindfolded, gagged with a knotted scarf and a head scarf is applied and tied tightly under the chin.

At this point I set a kitchen timer for a random amount of time between 30 to 60 minutes. Veronica is seated on the floor with her legs extended to the front. I then gag myself with a knotted scarf and use a pair of handcuffs, with the key attached by a string to the linking chain, to pinion my hands behind my back. Since I can see where I'm going, I slide over and sit next to Veronica, the side of our legs touching along our thighs.

The rules of this game go like this. Veronica is free to hold the switches of the vibrators on as much as she pleases. Here's the catch for her. If she has an orgasm before the kitchen timer rings, she loses. Veronica couldn't hide her climax if her life depended upon it. It's easy playing the spinning-out games with her, because the onset of her orgasm is telegraphed with a shuddering wave moving through her lower body, followed by a pretty good amount of hip heaving, deep breathing and moaning. Since I'm not blindfolded, she knows I'll spot it if she tries to cheat. On the other hand, seeing Veronica bound and working herself up is sometimes enough for me to come without any other stimulation. If I come before the timer goes off, I lose.

This situation puts Veronica on the horns of a dilemma; she can come closest to winning the game by keeping the vibrators humming (I can tell when they're running by sound and the movement of her body) — yet if she uses them too much, her passion will explode first. Prize in the game is the winner gets to keep the loser spread-eagled to the bed for the night and can use them for their own pleasure without being required to insure their orgasm.

Needless to say we only play this game on weekend or holiday nights, as both parties need some recovery time the next day. Again we observe one of our primary bondage safety rules in that the loser is not gagged during sleep periods, only during active times. They do spend the entire time blindfolded, usually with a head scarf applied so they can't rub off the blindfold on the pillow. We also leave a little slack in the limb bondage, since being tightly stretched to the corners of the bed for extended periods of time is just too uncomfortable. Both of us are good sports and don't try to get loose if we've lost the contest.

Veronica and I are interested in wooden bondage devices. Since neither of us has a place to keep dedicated bondage furniture I did the next best thing. I purchased a futon for my spare bedroom, giving us a wooden frame to work with. When it's in the bed form with the mattress in place it's just the right size for a comfortable spread-eagle. Without the mattress it makes a very versatile framework for fastening arms and legs in many interesting positions. All three of us are thinking up some new tie-ups for using the futon when it's in the sofa style.

Everyone's schedules have conspired to keep Brenda, Veronica and I from getting together much as a threesome. One time we got together we only had a short time to play. Brenda hadn't seen the futon yet so she stopped by one afternoon. All we had time for a was a quick tie-up, with vibrators providing the stimulation during the brief visit.

Both ladies stripped down to bra and panties and I tied their hands behind their backs, using a couple of scarves at the wrists and one at the elbows of each lady. They were gagged with one scarf pulled tightly between the teeth. Over this I placed a second scarf folded into a pad, and held it in place with a mouth covering scarf.

The futon was down in the bed form. I pulled it away from the wall and had Brenda kneel on the floor at the head end; Veronica did the same at the foot end. I spread each lady's legs apart and tied their thighs to the ends of the frame, using the slats under the mattress to insure separation of the legs. I then had them bend forward over the futon mattress and I pulled down their panties. I lubricated their vaginas and inserted a large vibrator with remote power switch into each lady. I pulled their panties up to hold the vibrators in place. I purposefully left them without blindfolds so they could watch each other as I cycled the vibrator power on and off.

Sometimes I left the vibrator turned off on one of them while I would vibrate the other one, massaging her breasts and clitoris from behind in full view of the unstimulated lady. Later, I gave the power switch on Brenda's vibrator to Veronica and vice-versa, giving them a chance to be in charge of each other's stimulation. Finally, I blindfolded the ladies and gave each the power switch to her own vibrator.

I moved back and forth between the ladies, massaging each lady's sensitive areas. Brenda finished first, and as she climaxed, I took the vibrator power switch away from Veronica, stopping her before she could achieve orgasm. I took off Brenda's gag and she willingly brought me to an orgasm orally.

I decided to leave Veronica tied and blindfolded until I could recharge and come again, although I did take off her gag. She started begging me to turn on her vibrator as she was feeling left high and dry. I loosened the scarves on Brenda's wrists and she finished untying herself and removed the vibrator from her love canal. When Brenda had finished releasing herself, I gave her the switch to Veronica's vibrator.

I climbed on the futon and positioned myself under Veronica. Brenda went around behind Veronica and pushed her forward, guiding her mouth down over my swollen member. Veronica began to energetically work her mouth as Brenda started cycling the vibrator on and off. Sometimes, Brenda would stop the vibrator and we would push Veronica back into the upright position. Brenda and I would then hug, kiss and rub each other close enough to Veronica that even with the blindfold she could tell what we were doing. This was particularly maddening to Veronica. When I was ready to come again, Veronica finished me orally while Brenda watched, this time allowing the vibrator to drive Veronica to a thundering conclusion.

Even though we haven't been able to coordinate schedules for the three of us often enough, Veronica and I did take a great trip with some friends of hers. A couple Veronica knows have a place at the Lake of the Ozarks. It's not just a cabin, but a lakefront, three bedroom, two bath year-round type house with a boat dock and two boats.

With our busy schedules we just had from Friday afternoon to Saturday evening available to us before we had to return home. We were able to leave just after lunch Friday, getting us to the lake by mid-afternoon. Our hosts were going to arrive quite a bit later that evening. When I picked up Veronica at her house, I could sense that even though her friends were not people we could share our interest in bondage with, this was still going to be a special weekend.

The weather had just turned cool and Veronica was wearing a tan trench coat. A scarf tied in the knotted bib style was tucked into the neckline of the coat. She was wearing a really sexy pair of patterned hose with stylish short boots. Her hair and make-up were especially tastefully done. To look at her, she seemed to be the essence of a career woman, very professional looking indeed. She was carrying one of her favorite designer handbags, an oversize model with a shoulder strap. What was in that handbag was another matter altogether.

About halfway to the lake Veronica told me to pull over at a scenic little picnic area, instructing me to park the car so the passenger side was nearest the road. As usual nobody was using the area and traffic on the road was zooming past. When I stopped the car Veronica told me she wanted to give me a preview of what I could expect to get when we got to the lake. With that comment she turned her body toward me and opened up the front of the trench coat to reveal her outfit. Except for the garter belt, hose, coat, scarf and shoes she was only wearing her birthday suit.

We engaged in a little heavy petting and when I was aroused enough to invite her to the back seat she abruptly detached herself from my embrace and buttoned up her coat. She told me I was getting a preview, not the feature presentation. I would get the whole show when we got to the lake. Needless to say the rest of the trip seemed to take an eternity, even though I was driving above the speed limit.

When we got to the lake I took Veronica into the house quickly and we finished what we started earlier with an afternoon of steamy love-making. We finished well before our hosts arrived. I figured that was it for sex that weekend but it had already been great fun and was more than I was expecting.

As I said earlier, our hosts are not people with whom Veronica and I would share any intimate details of our relationship. The bedroom we were going to use was rather small, dominated by a full size bed with brass head and foot boards. Naturally my mind wandered to the many ways we could use the bed for bondage but I wasn't expecting to get to try any of them on this trip. The bedroom was next to the large family room. The family room held a big screen television, lots of comfortable furniture and a massive stone fireplace, making the family room the center of activity in the house. Like many of the older homes at the lake it was built without a lot of thought to modern ventilation techniques. Our bedroom had a simple pass through type vent directly into the family room to facilitate air movement. The acoustics of the rooms transmitted anything more than a whisper straight through the wall into the adjacent room. This wasn't a great set-up for privacy.

We spent the evening with Veronica's friends playing cards, doing a little night dock fishing, drinking a big pitcher of "sex-on-the-beach' and enjoying a lot of pleasant conversation in front of the fireplace. After midnight, Veronica and I excused ourselves to the bedroom, refilling our drink glasses on the way. Our hosts were staying up a little later to catch a movie, leaving them in the family room. As we were leaving they moved over to the floor near the fireplace instead of on the couch next to the wall of our bedroom. This gave us a little more breathing space since noise didn't travel quite as well across the family room. They might have wanted to be closer to the fireplace or maybe they were just trying to be considerate.

Veronica likes to share a pair of pajamas with me, so she undressed and put on the top, while I got the bottoms. After Veronica locked the bedroom door she came to bed. I noticed she was bringing her handbag over next to the bed. I passed this off as an instinctive habit from her frequent job related travels and stays in unfamiliar hotels. She slid into the bed and cuddled up close.

I wrapped my arms around her and pulled her tightly to me. She placed her mouth close to my ear and quietly whispered to me. It seems she thought she had been a bad girl by showing herself to me and getting me aroused out on the way to the lake. She thought I might want to give her a little payback for the stunt on the highway. When I whispered back an affirmative reply, she pulled a bundle of her own scarves from the handbag. Veronica also has an extensive collection of scarves but we usually use mine for bondage since her scarves are a fundamental part of her wardrobe.

This trip I hadn't brought any of my sex toys since I didn't know we were going to be able to play fun games. Quickly and quietly I tied her wrists and ankles to the head and foot of the bed, fastening her in a narrow spread-eagle off to one side of the bed. This left me enough room to lay next to her. Since we couldn't afford for her to make any noise, an effective gag was imperative. First I packed a medium square scarf into Veronica's mouth. Next I pulled a knotted scarf deep between her teeth and tied it behind her head. Over this I tied two mouth covering scarves, one of them a large oblong which I wrapped around her head several times over the knotted scarf. I finished off with a head covering scarf tied tightly under the chin. I decided not to blindfold her as I wanted her to be able to watch the things I was going to do to her.

I unbuttoned the pajama top and started to work Veronica's sensitive parts with some gentle skin massage. Later, I stepped up the pace to include a deeper massage and began to work her breasts with my mouth. Then I moved on to her pubic region with both hands and mouth. In my last letter I told you how sexy we found the blindfold-ice cube scene in the movie 9 ½ Weeks. Even without the blindfold, when I apply ice cubes to Veronica's skin, nipples, vulva and clitoris during foreplay we both get aroused. I took some cubes from our drinks and rubbed them in all the right spots, gently licking the drink residue from the ice off Veronica's skin adding to the sensation.

Even with the extensive gag Veronica could, of course, still make enough noise to be heard in the family room. Keeping quiet during our passion was a major effort for both of us and we really couldn't afford to make the bed shake either. I could tell from looking at Veronica the gag was somewhat uncomfortable, even though she wasn't saying so or asking to be let loose. I decided to let her off easy to avoid the possible embarrassment of discovery, finishing her orally after just fifteen or twenty minutes.

I took my pleasure during intercourse in a decidedly non-traditional missionary position with Veronica still gagged and bound to the bed. I was so aroused that I didn't have to worry about making too much noise or shaking the bed as it only took short strokes to bring on my orgasm. I came quickly and as I did I buried my face between Veronica's breasts, squeezing them tightly to my cheeks and over my mouth to muffle any sounds I might be making.

I untied Veronica, we put the scarves back into the handbag and both dropped off to a deep, satisfying sleep. The next morning, we went for a delightful boat ride on the lake with our hosts before departing for home. The morning was chilly and Veronica wore a scarf folded into a triangle, wrapped over her head, the ends crossed and pulled around her neck, tying them at the back of her head over the point of the scarf. This style is one of my favorite sophisticated looks and is great for keeping Veronica's hair in place. We hugged and kissed frequently during the boat ride and Veronica's friends commented about how much we seemed to care for each other. That weekend turned out to be more fun than I could have ever expected.

Hopefully we can get some more play time with Brenda.

From 'J' in the Midwest

Dear Harmony,

The beautiful blonde was breathing heavily through the stocking gag as I stepped back to admire my work.

Vanessa had given me a strange, quizzical look when I had produced the black long sleeved scooped neck leotard and suggested that she slip into it. She gave me an even stranger look when she stepped back into the room wearing it and found me wearing a white stocking mask, tight white T-shirt and white panty hose.

Before she could react, I pulled her quickly into me and stuffed a nylon stocking into her mouth and secured it with a second nylon which I tied behind her neck. My gamble was paying off since she was obviously enjoying the situation. I placed one hand on her left breast and the other down between her thighs. As I massaged her like that, I told her that I was going to tie her up and make rape fantasy love to her. Her low gurgling moan gave me the permission I needed to tie her wrists behind her securely with a stocking.

I completed her bondage by pulling another stocking down over her head. She was moaning and writhing passionately and I descended onto her and made both of us feel loved to a degree we had never attained before.

Anonymous

Do women enjoy being tied up? A lot depends on the finesse of the person doing the tying. Some women like tying up other women, of course, and there are many different preferences. But as to whether or not the woman enjoys it or is just a reluctant participant pressured into it by a dominant male with sexist attitudes; when you have tied up a particular woman hundreds of times, and gagged her on more than fifty occasions, and she has never once asked you to desist, and when, on one occasion, after requesting to be untied in order to visit the bathroom, she returns with the gag still firmly wedged between her teeth, and then she stands with her back to you and presents her hands to be tied again as before, does this sound like something forced on an unwilling participant?

Just to be sure, however, in case I had been mistaken, one night I asked Victoria straight out what she thought. "You haven't told me why you like having your hands tied behind your back." I put this to her as we were lying in bed together after a particularly torrid session. She wrinkled her brow thoughtfully for a moment, then smiled. "Well," she said, without equivocation, "it takes away your control, and... and... it thrusts your breasts forward!"

Amoroso, Australia

From my experience, the demeanor most arousing is that of curiosity in the eyes of a friend who has just had her wrists tied and her mouth gagged for the first time, and realizes "Hey, this may be interesting!

The more intelligent and capable a lady is the better bondage partner she can be. She knows that this is a loving — rather than adversarial — situation. She may appreciate the temporary respite from her responsibilities. Sometimes the immobility, denial of speech, and blindfolding allows restorative withdrawal into a meditation-like focus on the puzzle of her bondage.

With an educated sense of humor and self-confidence, it's fun to recognize the pleasure she has granted the bondager to whom she is entrusted, and that he is, ironically, no less a "prisoner of love" than herself.

Max in Maryland

You wield that subtle power of submission that rules my desire and my same desire is what controls you now— You hold me captive with your beauty. I hold you captive with my rope as I attend every word you cannot speak, you silently acquiesce to my overpowering passion, the circular passions reciprocate while you surrender helplessly to satisfy me and I lust to satiate that flame within you like the bonds that encircle you now.

This loving game we play has no winner or loser. It always ends up in a tie.

Jon Woods

FROM HER POINT OF VIEW:

This is excerpted from a brief survey several years ago. These answers shed soft light on the perspective of some females on bondage.

Before you began actively participating, did you ever show any interest in bondage beforehand?

Yes — in fantasies...

Yes — I was intrigued by handcuffs, four-poster beds, etc.

Yes — I always wished I was Sky King's daughter.

Is what you know now different from what you first thought bondage was about?

Yes — Yes, its purpose is not to cause pain.

Yes — I found it is not dangerous. I'm not scared.

When you are tied, what feelings are you most aware of?

I'm where I belong.

What for you is the best aspect of bondage?

I feel my husband needs and loves me.

We have been married ten years. I let him tie me up because the look of total adoration in his eyes makes it worthwhile and shows how much he truly loves me.

WELL, YES, WE HAVE GIVEN THIS SOME THOUGHT

WHY BONDAGE LOOKS GOOD

By B. D. Smith

She's bound and gagged: the very phrase initiates the spell. When we wrap her tightly in cord, coiling it around her wrists and breasts and ankles, and between her thighs, we enfold and protect her with our own limbs, transformed and symbolized.

When we pack her mouth with cloth and pull a scarf tight over soft lips, we represent our own mouths and tongues and create a kiss that can last forever.

Bondage delights our eyes and enchants our hearts because the bonds and gag that hold our heroine symbolize the embrace of our passionate love, frozen in time.

And so a connection is made at last — a first step toward understanding this unusual pleasure of ours, how something seen by our eyes can feel so good in our souls. Someone has finally explained to us the psychic link between something seen and something felt.

WHY BONDAGE LOOKS GOOD

By K. H., Texas

First, a woman in bondage represents mystery, at its most romantic and enigmatic. The woman is gagged and bound. How has this come to be? How was it done? And why?

Second, a bound woman radiates awareness. It seems as though every nerve in her body is alive to its fullest, as she is made aware of every little motion and sound around her. To those who say her bondage reduces a woman's status to that of a mere object, I say: look at the eyes. That's not the story they tell.

Lastly, and perhaps most importantly, the best of the bondage photos convey that most noble of human attributes, trust. Victims do not attract me, not in the least. The woman must be a partner in the proceedings, perhaps even the instigator. A woman must trust someone very much to surrender herself so fully and so physically to that person. It is very easy to draw sexual overtones to the concept of bondage, and I would be foolish to try to deny that they exist.

As soon as we see the tied and gagged woman, we see possibility. She represents unlimited potential. Before she is bound she has choice, to consent, to resist. Once she is freed she has choice again, to proceed or refuse. While she is bound, she has surrendered options. She belongs. It is a moment of pure owning. She looks good because we understand that fleeting truth, identify the force and responsibility of that choice, and recognize that power, that intrinsic realization of pure romance.

WHY BONDAGE LOOKS GOOD

By Richard, Oklahoma

Bondage looks good because it is part of the age-old visual language of Romance. It is pleasing to the eye of a man because it satisfies the primitive hunter urge in him—and the noblest part of that: the need for the triumph of capture.

Provided duress is absent, it pleases the eye of a woman because it satisfies a deep longing to be completely taken in love and owned (though for her what is felt is often more important than what is seen). Passion, sympathy, sensuous envy, power and pleasure are feelings and emotions that men and women associate with bondage when they see it.

Bondage is interesting and it is intriguing. To evoke such feelings and emotions, and to capture human attention as it does in the still photograph and the cinema, bondage must look good.!!!

WHY BONDAGE LOOKS GOOD

By Sarah Foster Tate, Australia

A woman who is visually rendered powerless and dependent will, if nothing else, gain a man's attention. He is designed to react, and he will. If the man sees the woman as looking good, then he is reacting instinctively. It is pure, very right, and although not every individual experiences this same thing, it is quite how it should be.

Bondage also looks good because it takes a woman back to her primal basics. She is completely dependent, vulnerable, and totally owned by her man. All traditional virtues, which are glaringly accentuated by rope. There is no evading the helplessness. And when a woman truly feels that helplessness, you are likely to witness her feeling emotions and giving expressions that you have never seen her feel or give before. She will look beautiful.

The emotions in her eyes which are so attractive are enhanced by masking the lower part of her face

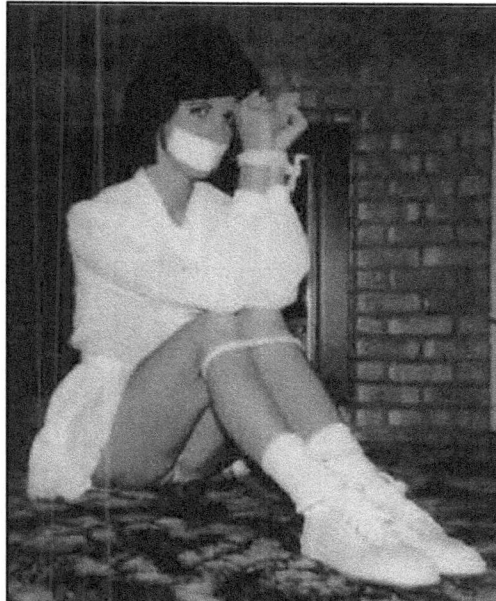

with a gag. She is transformed beyond being a woman, to being the idealized woman. All vulnerability and big expressive eyes — sometimes defiant or playfully demanding, but she is still vulnerable woman. Her elbows tied together will make her breasts seem rounder and fuller. A corset or rope cinches her waist, while all the traditionally slim parts of the body: wrists, ankles and knees are bound, leaving the rest of her soft skin to curve slightly over the ropes.

Bondage is an inside experience for the woman and an outside experience for the man. It looks good because bondage physically enhances the shape of her body, because the emotions in her eyes are those that a man is triggered to respond to, and because she is everything a woman should be — something to own, to protect, to desire, and to love.

WHY BONDAGE LOOKS GOOD

By J. C., Australia

First, the image of the female in constraint is virtually archetypal in our culture. Andromeda chained to her rock with arms outspread as sacrifice to the sea-monster, proud Hippolyta surrendering first to Heracles and later to Theseus; Psyche, Europe, Persephone...the list of ladies who were conquered or abducted for their beauty is virtually endless, and is still being added to by our creative writers.

In each case the image is similar...a lovely lady, helpless, desirable and precious. A lady worth fighting

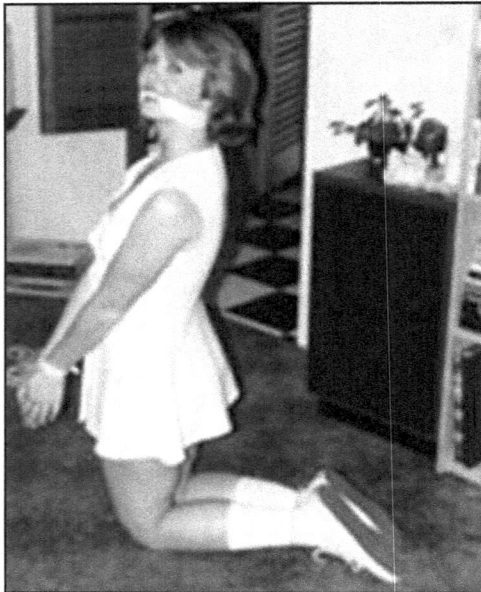

for, holding against all comers, and cherishing. And, in our own terms, a lady worth defying social convention for. She is the captive princess, the slave goddess of all our daydreams, and the lady's submission is also a pyrrhic conquest by her of the captor.

The female is expected to be as beautiful as she can be, and is encouraged by society to adorn and paint herself, to captiously vary her image season by season, and generally create a mystery and miracle of herself...one day a gamin, the next a sophisticate; one day adorned like a princess, the next in battle fatigues like a leftover from Che Guevara's guerillas...yet always desirable. And where there is desire there will be pursuit, and where there is pursuit there will be capture.

Let those who wish to do so engineer their conquests through polite societal forms of courtship and acquiescence. We prefer a more overt image of surrender and submission, and to us the image of bondage will always be the most beautiful face of love.

PART FIVE
When Bondage and Sex Intersect...

TIME NOW FOR SOME WELL-CONCEIVED FICTION, EROTICALLY RENDERED!

Gloria Hendricks sucked the fresh, cool air deep into her lungs as she stood on the slope above the lake. Brilliant sunlight winked off its blue water, and the wind whispered loudly in the fall-bright leaves of the trees. The same breeze caressed her long hair, stirring its bronze-colored locks gently, and her gray eyes glistened as pleasure and anticipation flooded through her. Her blood bubbled through her veins, alive and vibrant as Jack stood beside her.

"It's gorgeous, Jack!" she exclaimed breathlessly. "I've never seen anything so beautiful."

"I have," he said softly, and took her in his arms. Their lips met long and lingeringly, tongues mating in fire as the Indian Summer sun beat down.

"Gee," she sighed as they finally broke the kiss, her fingers stroking his back through his shirt as he caressed the firm curve of her tight, worn denims. "Why didn't we ever come up here before?"

"Because," Jack grinned, "we didn't own the place then. I only managed to buy it back last month, you know."

She nodded against his chest. The cabin above them had belonged to Jack's grandfather, but it had been sold to someone else long ago. Getting it back had been something of an obsession with him, and, looking at the beauty which surrounded it, she could understand why.

"But it's so isolated," she sighed again, nuzzling his throat.

"Yeah, that's the beauty of it," Jack chuckled, achieving a lewd smirk.

"Of course, during the summer we'll have neighbors…about a half a mile that way," he pointed east "… and about three-quarters of a mile the other way. But all the summer people have gone; we've got it all to ourselves."

"I know, wicked man," she murmured, grabbing his ears and pulling him down to kiss again. He responded enthusiastically, then broke away again.

"Enough, wench! You know why we came. And," he added significantly, "we better start pretty soon. The sun'll go down in about four hours, and we don't want to waste it. Things are going to get a little chilly once it's gone."

"You're sure no one's going to see us?" Gloria asked, the tiniest flicker of nervousness mingling with the anticipation in her brilliant eyes.

"I can't absolutely guarantee it," he said, "— that's part of the thrill, isn't it? But no one's living here on the lake right this minute."

"I guess that's good enough," she agreed, and then smiled brilliantly. "And you're right. It is part of the thrill."

"Then let's show you the cabin and find you a place to change into something sexy," he said, taking her suitcase and leading her up the path to the cabin with an arm around her trim waist. "Something real sexy, I hope."

"I'll turn your bones to water, lover," Gloria promised darkly, her eyes flashing fire with the words.

"Great. I'll hold you to that—and promise you something to really get you into the swing of things in honor of it," Jack promised softly.

The cabin was simply but comfortably furnished and the bedroom boasted a full-length triple mirror. Gloria shucked out of her blouse and jeans, then peeled off her lingerie to stand naked before the three panels, admiring her trio of selves. She cupped her naked breasts gently massaging her nipples and purring to herself at the delicious sensations which answered. Then she lowered her hands with a firm assertion of will to turn to the ruffles and bows and silk and satin filling her open suitcase. She selected her garments with care, feeling the inner tension quivering higher and higher as she made her choices. She and Jack had been into bondage games for over three years now, but this would be a first. An experience they had never quite dared try before — and she was determined to look her absolute best for it.

She laid her chosen garments carefully over the back of a chair and opened her cosmetics case, seating herself before the old-fashioned dressing table. She applied her makeup carefully, then turned and studied her reflection and made a few final adjustments, half-stunned by the raw, sultry sensuality she had evoked, then applied body perfume lavishly. Armpits and breasts, thighs and crotch — all were anointed with the low-key yet somehow sizzling scent Jack had given her for her birthday. As a final touch, she opened the small jar of rouge and carefully painted the bold circles of her areolas and nipples. They winked at her—scarlet and impudent, sinfully erotic in the mirror.

She studied herself once more, turning on her toes and approving the devastating appearance she had created. Then she donned the garments she had laid out: white lace garter belt, white nylons, tiny satin panties, their front panel marked with a deep v-shaped cutout that plunged so far the rich bronze silk of her crotch erupted through it. She stroked the curls lightly for a moment, then shook free of the auto-eroticism of her own touch with a soft chuckle and reached for the corselet.

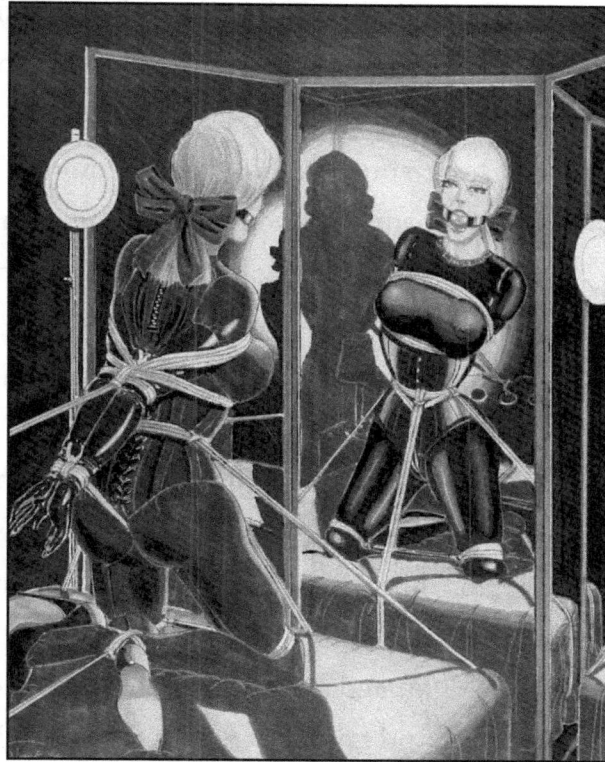

Jack had never seen any of her new garments, and she was looking forward to the effect of that corselet. She fastened its soft silk about her; its un-stayed tightness lifted and separated her naked breasts, pushing them even higher, making them even more poutingly prominent and delicious. She was delighted; it looked even sexier than it had in the fitting room mirror when she first tried it on.

As a final garnish, she slipped on the elbow length evening gloves of white, brocaded silk and fastened her five-inch strap-on heels. She shrugged into her white satin housecoat and stepped out into a spill of windowed sunlight to face her waiting husband.

Jack's eyes moved over her face with something like awe. She had been experimenting with cosmetics for several months, but this was the best she had yet achieved, and they both knew it.

Gloria smiled hungrily at him as she eyed his obviously swelling crotch. If he thought this looked good, she thought wickedly, just wait until he saw the rest of her outfit!

"Don't you just look good enough to eat," he said finally, his voice very soft. "Lordy, but you've outdone yourself this time, Glor!"

"Why thank you, oh Lord and Master," she simpered, pouting prettily.

"And I can tell from your expression you've got something even better under than housecoat," Jack said, still softly. "So why hide it?"

"Now?" She licked her lips against a quaver of nervousness. "Don't you want to wait till we get where we're going?"

"No," he said softly. "It's not far, and I want to see you. I want to see you looking beautiful and sexy in the sunlight all the way there."

She glanced out the window at the empty woods and the rich sunlight on red and gold leaves, then back to her husband's face and nodded slowly, the fire in her gray eyes rising higher as her hands went to her sash. Satin whispered as she unbelted the robe and shrugged it down her shoulders, standing before him in all of her delicate and vulnerable loveliness. Jack's eyes widened in astonished delight and approval. "Oh my God," he whispered.

"You like me?" Gloria asked. She meant for her voice to come out pert and snippy; it actually came out soft and tenderly loving.

"Do I like you? Like you?!" He took her in his arms and kissed her, letting the urgent fire of his mouth answer her. Her arms went around his neck, drawing his head even more firmly down to her, and she felt her thighs weaken. She had told him she would turn his bones to water, and she had; she had not fully realized how his reaction would affect her. It was Jack who finally pulled away with a shaken little laugh.

"Watch it," he chided gently. "I don't plan to dump you down on the floor right here and now, Gloria. I promised you something extra special, and, believe me, you're going to get it."

"I am?" she purred, panting with her own desire and not sure whether she was disappointed or elated by the delay.

"You are," he said firmly, and opened his duffel bag to draw out a black, ring-studded leather collar.

Gloria stared at it avidly, the blowtorch in her belly clicking up another notch. She held her head very erect, her eyes locked smolderingly to his as he slipped the high, smooth leather about her slender throat. He buckled it, its heavy rings flashing, and Gloria swallowed a moan of arousal and anticipation as the glove-smooth leather clasped her. Jack moved around behind her, the soft, white cotton rope gleaming in his hands.

Gloria stood arrow-straight, sweat prickling on her skin, smelling the strengthening sweetness of her body perfume as her skin warmed and flushed tinglingly.

The rope circled her wrists gently -- firmly imprisoning them. He didn't bind them together; instead, he bound them separately to rings on the back of her collar. She shuddered in delight as her hands were imprisoned behind her neck, opening her arms to frame her head, lifting her breasts still higher and arching her spine sweetly. The sensation of vulnerability and sweet, sweet surrender ached in her flesh, rising as it always rose. His ropes rendered her captive in his hands, subject to whatever delight he had planned for her. She wore them willingly, eagerly, recognizing them as emblems of her preciousness.

Jack reached back into the duffel bag to produce a thick, cushioned leather bit gag and Gloria's eyes flared. It was one of her favorites; she loved the way its heavy severity garnished her helpless appearance, yet it was actually mild enough for extended wear. It muffled without silencing, rendered her wordless without rendering her mute, and filled her mouth without limiting her breath. She bent her head forward eagerly as Jack applied and adjusted it, and, when he released her, shook her head like a newly-bridled horse, tasting the leather-flavored fullness of her mouth with delight.

Jack smiled into her glowing eyes and leaned forward, kissing her forehead gently and then moving lower to kiss her eyelids and lick her cheeks along the upper edge of the gag-strap, as she purred. Then he lifted his mouth away and snapped the chain leash to her collar.

The sharp little "snick" as the snap-hook closed was the final preliminary. It announced the beginning of the great experiment, and she moved behind him with butterflies of tremulous anticipation and nervousness beating the inside of her belly as he shouldered the duffel bag and led her slowly out the front door into the brilliant sunlight of early afternoon.

Gloria stepped out the door and the sunlight stabbed her, laying its warmth over her skin. She moaned into the gag, quivering in momentary bliss, her mind teeming with confusing and conflicting thoughts. She had never been bound outside before, and the strangeness of it largely explained the sudden flash of pleasure. But there was more to it. The sense of doing something forbidden, of violating the taboos which said such games should be played only within the shielding privacy of four walls, was part of it. So was the slight chill in the air, tweaking at her nipples even as the warmth of the sunlight enfolded her.

But strongest of all was the sense of exposure, of vulnerability, of the gnawing, delightfully titillating possibility that Jack was wrong — that they would turn a corner or come out from around a tree and find themselves face-to-face with some birdwatcher or hiker. She moaned, clasping her satin thighs together even as she stumbled docilely along behind her husband. Damn! Oh, damn! Jack had promised her a treat, yet she had never dreamed just being bound outside could have such a powerful erotic effect!

Jack led her toward some well-remembered goal with gentle tugs on the leash and she followed happily, wallowing in the sensual tide which washed over her. Sweat gleamed on her golden skin like silver dust as her juices woke to ever more clamorous life. It was difficult to walk over the uneven ground with her wrists lashed behind her neck, but Jack went very slowly, letting her pick her way with a delicate, hesitant gait which lent a hormone-popping, swaying sensuality to her movement. She didn't walk — she undulated through the sun and shade-patched woods in her ropes and collar, towed along on her leash, her mouth salivating around the gag.

She followed him in a sensual daze, and she was none too clear on how far they had gone when Jack came to the edge of a clearing and paused. She paused behind him, panting and sweating, quivering with lust and the delightful knowledge that she would be left to quiver as he tightened the screws of passion ever tighter—slowly, oh soooo slowly!—until he was ready for her to come.

The explosion would be all the stronger, focused down to an H-bomb burst of passion by his long, slow tantalization of her captive flesh. She felt her need clawing at her, urging her on, driving her to seek the explosion — yet at the same time she hoped that he would deny her skillfully far past the point she believed she could endure.

She blinked her eyes into focus as they stood in the dappled shade patterns at the edge of the clearing. A single, mammoth beech tree dominated the center of the clearing. A heavy branch thrust out twelve feet above the ground, supporting two frayed ropes and an ancient, weather beaten swing. Gloria stared at it, panting, as she tried to reason out what

Jack had planned for her sensual torment and delight here where he had played as a child. He gave no sign as he leashed her to a slender-trunked dogwood at the edge of the clearing.

Then he pulled her against him, pressing his swollen crotch against her. She groaned in pleasure, then whined in delighted frustration as he stopped just before she could climax. He laughed at her lovingly, stroking her fevered cheek gently, and then walked away from her. She whined again, loudly, begging him to return even while they both knew that was the last thing she truly wished. He ignored her entreaties with an impudent grin and lowered his eyes, searching through the leaves for something.

She wondered what, but she knew he would tell her — or show her — only when he was ready, so she concentrated instead on the delightful lust rippling through her sweating, scantily-clad flesh like ocean waves. He suddenly stooped and straightened with a dead branch, thick as his wrist, absolutely straight and over four feet long. He tested it for soundness and nodded his satisfaction, then strolled back to her. She whined questioningly around the gag, querying his intent in the only way she could, her nerves quivering with delight as her question came out wordlessly. The light in his eyes said he understood, but it also said that he wouldn't tell her.

He unleashed her from the dogwood and led her to stand beside the ancient swing. When he dropped the leash to hang heavily between her breasts, the chill chain stroking their sweating inner swells, Gloria's wet thighs trembled. Jack's grin widened and he wrinkled his nose teasingly at the smell of her lust, and Gloria blushed prettily, deliciously embarrassed by the proof of her need.

He knelt and noosed soft rope around one ankle, lashing it to the end of his branch, then pushed her feet so wide that she swayed for balance as he lashed her other foot to the other end. She groaned delicately past her gag as the tendons tensed in her crotch, opening her slim, golden legs vulnerably wide while cool forest air kissed her inner thighs like a feathery lash.

He chuckled at her sound and ran another length of rope around the base of her left thigh, drawing it firmly up into the angle of her crotch. He passed the rope up over the swell of her hip and around her back, then across her pelvis, back behind her right hip and down around her right thigh. She quivered as his hands and rope brushed her, peering down over her pouting, quivering breasts as he repeated the process five times, forming a wide girdle of rope around her thighs and across her hips and the small of her back without once crossing the front or back of her panties. Her lust-curdled mind tried to understand its purpose — particularly in the absence of a crotch rope.

The puzzle was momentarily chased from her mind as he stood once more and fresh ropes cinched her bent arms firmly, locked into the sharp bend already imposed by binding her wrists to the back of her collar, and tied a cord around her bound, gloved wrists. She moaned in delighted mystery as he untied her separate wrist ropes from her collar and threaded the new cord's looped end loosely through a single ring on its very back. Another, much longer cord went through the bottom of the loop, and then he eased her down to sit in the crumbly-dry beech leaves.

Gloria shuddered in delight, the fire in her center burning higher with every passing instant of captivity. The dry leaves, gently pricking her bare skin or slickly stiff through her thin satin panties, jolted her like tiny electric sparks. The cool, leaf-smelling air whispered over her sweat-slicked skin on the teeth of a tiny breeze, its near-chill an exquisite counterbalance to the raging heat within her flesh.

Sunlight and shade and the rustle of leaves danced in her blood like lightning. The burning, bubbling heat of her physical sensations was stabbed through and through by the unending delicacy of fear — fear that someone would come, fear that someone would see, fear that someone would learn their secret...and anticipation of the delightful, mind-curdling embarrassment which would, she knew, drive her into instant orgasm if she felt a stranger's eyes ...

She was so enveloped in the giddy tides of sensation and anticipation swirling through her that she didn't notice Jack throwing a coil of rope over the beech limb so far above her. She still hadn't noticed when he eased her to lie on her back, her bound elbows and ripe, sweat-soaked breasts thrusting towards the blue sky showing through the leaves, and looped the rope from her wrists around the center of the branch between her feet.

She twitched and jerked in delight as he drew on the rope, pulling her legs back, arching her back, thrusting her hips upwards. Abruptly her thighs tensed, the muscles knotted, and then she gasped as a lightning climax flashed through her, throwing her into shuddering, twitching spasms. Each bite of pleasure staggered her nerves — yet she knew from long, delightful experience that this was only a shadow of what was to come. The orgasm which awaited her would be an earthquake of passion!

Jack tied the rope finally, her heels under her ass, her knees sharply bent so that her legs were doubled. It was mildly strenuous and thoroughly blissful as her burning, shuddering crotch pressed against the tightened panel of her panties and the thigh ropes of her girdle gnawed into her straining groin. Then she felt something plucking at the front of that same rope girdle and opened glazed eyes, trying futilely to lift her head and see. She couldn't see the point of attachment, but she could see the rope dangling from the tree limb above her head and twitching as he tied it.

Her eyes widened in disbelief and delight as she guessed what he was about to do. He tested all his knots carefully, then smiled down into her fuming eyes as he heaved slowly and steadily on the hanging rope.

Gloria warbled in ecstasy as the rope girdle answered the lift of the rope, plucking her ass off her heels, lifting her. She rose into the air slowly, spinning in slow circles as she left the ground. The carefully arranged girdle distributed the lifting pressure, drawing tighter and gnawing into her without binding or pinching. Her own weight drew the ropes tight, but Jack had placed them so cunningly that their tiny edge of discomfort was minute, just strong enough to stroke her pleasure with added bite.

He drew her upward until her feet were off the ground, her crotch conveniently raised to waist level on him, her body arched sharply back. She groaned deep in her throat, the weight of her breasts rolling on her chest, her pulse stuttering in her stony nipples and throbbing in her hanging temples. She couldn't lift her head to see a single thing he might choose to do, and her uncertainty fueled her excitement, for the only thing of which she was certain was that whatever he did would be delightful. Then she felt his hands on her straining belly, stroking and caressing, toying with her. She quivered and jerked, instinctively humping her hips, and her involuntary response sent her swaying like a pendulum, swaying below the tree limb like a child's swing. She whined around her gag, begging him to pull her panties aside, but he only chuckled, his fingers like feathers on her smoking flesh, and she moaned in blissful frustration as her passion blazed totally out of her control.

And when he did touch her panties, it was not to remove them. She moaned in confusion as she felt him pluck them up and away from her then grunted and gasped in surprised pleasure as he slid the butterfly vibrator down inside them, adjusting it with fiendish care before he switched it on, feeling the magma gather within her, sobbing as she fought to resist it, to savor every last ounce of anticipation and smoking hunger. But Jack knew exactly what was passing through her, and he laughed lovingly as he moved around her hanging body and gently unpinned her braided hair.

She gasped and moaned, begging for release even as she fought it, her body twitching and jerking, fighting her bonds against her will as the pleasure scoured her like a lash of flame. And then he produced a long, stiff feather, standing beside her and holding her gently motionless by her braid as the feather danced across her sweat-soaked nipples.

She lurched and gasped and moaned around the gag. She wailed as the tiny brush of the feather broke the last barrier and hurled her into a maelstrom of fire. She vibrated as orgasm exploded within her. She wailed through the eternity of orgasm, an eternity of mind-shattering pleasure she could not endure. And yet she did endure it. Her wild, keening song of gagged bliss ended slowly, dying into a slow, sighing croon of aftermath and tenderness as she stared up at her husband through glazed gray eyes shadowed with love and passion.

Jack smiled tenderly down at her and bent to kiss her breasts, licking the sweet salt of her pleasure sweat from them, and she shuddered afresh at the hot, wet kiss of his tongue. Her hips shifted, the vibrator still buzzing against her. Her eyes widened as she felt the tide within begin to rise once more, and Jack laughed softly, twirling his feather across her nipples again.

"Like my old swing tree?" he whispered, and she groaned softly, nodding her head dazedly. "I thought you would — and the best is yet to come." She blinked and he laughed more loudly. "Oh, yes, honey. You won't believe how many times you're going to come this afternoon. And then, when you've felt it all, it's my turn to share it with you. I imagine your position's going to make it very interesting indeed, then — don't you?"

Gloria's eyes smiled up at him above her gag, even as her hips rolled slowly and lustfully within their girdle of cords and the rope to the limb above creaked. She nodded enthusiastically, moaning as the pleasure rose once more.

"After all," Jack chuckled, tickling her shrewdly, "I did promise you we'd get you into the swing of things, didn't I, dear?"

HAPPY ENDING!

Ahhhh from the TV speakers, and Elaine Vaughn wiggled in embarrassment.

A sudden squeal followed, and she shut her eyes, her face burning, for there would be no more sighs for the next half hour, and the squeals would grow ever more frantic and pleading. She knew. They were hers. She squirmed as her sounds grew shriller, but her present bondage was as inescapable as it was elegantly uncomplicated.

She knelt, naked, by the TV in her leather wrist and ankle cuffs. Her ankles were crossed, secured by a steel rod through the cuffs' metal rings. The eyelet at the rod's end was padlocked to an eyebolt between her toes, and her arms were folded behind her, wrist cuffs pinned above one another by sliding the same rod through their rings and, in the final step which perfected her bondage, the smaller eyelet atop the rod was snap-hooked to the back of her tall collar.

She could slide her wrists up and down the rod, but that was all she could do. If she could raise one hand — just one! — as high as the snap-hook at her collar, she could be free, but she could just barely get the tip on one thumb that high, and a thumb in isolation was not enough. She was neatly, inescapably fastened, and the rod was short enough to arch her spine in a sharp bend that woke quivering strain in her thighs and belly. But this was bondage after all, and delicious as gentle, nibbling love play was, occasional rigor was important too. Or it was for her, and she knew her bondager was too big a pussycat to do anything harsh...which was why she could enjoy such strenuous moments.

Her recorded squeals rose a notch and her belly jerked as she panted in delicious embarrassment. She wished she could see the screen, but confined as she was, all she could see (assuming she ever stopped blushing long enough to look) would be Duncan's happy eyes, savoring the bondage which had been while he looked forward to that which was to be. It didn't matter. She'd already seen the tape of her gagged face, and nude body, spread-eagled for his lips and tongue, squealing and bucking under his vibrator and feather. She'd already seen herself slippery and gleaming with sweat, spastic with lust as she fought her straps in a frenzy of passion.

Her recorded sounds grew louder yet. Soon, she knew, they would become an imploring madness— frantic and pleading, yet rendered wordless and futile by the fat ball in her mouth. The same ball she sucked now, moaning as hot, thick wetness welled slowly down her tanned thighs and her trapped tongue tasted the countless marks her teeth had made in the past three years.

Elaine Hodgkins had known about male desire since she turned thirteen, for she was slim and petite, with brown hair so dark it was almost black and skin like shadowed cream. Her oval face just missed being beautiful, but she'd always known she was more than pretty, with huge brown eyes and a sleek, sinuous grace that went well with her high, firm breasts and dainty waist.

None of which prevented her first marriage from being a disaster. Not that it had been her fault, though it had taken years for her to truly believe that. Unfortunately, all she'd seen at the start was a gorgeous face and physique wrapped around a college football star named Jason Harder.

Jason was a graduating senior and she a lowly freshman, so his interest in her was devastatingly flattering. He talked her out of her virginity with absurd ease (though to be fair, she'd been eager for him to do that) and into dropping out to marry him with only slightly more difficulty. Of course, she hadn't realized — then — how very little there was inside the lovely package.

She found out all too soon. Jason was arrogant, self-centered and cruel. His casual, constant put-downs had chipped away at her self-esteem in a way she'd once assumed was unintentional. But she suspected now that he'd known all along that she was brighter than him and chose to deny it to them both. Whatever his reason his thousands of slighting references to the career dreams she'd shelved to wed him slowly turned to fleeting contempt...and worse.

But it wasn't until Jennifer was born that he first struck her. If not for Jennifer, she would have left him - or so she thought. It was hard to be sure, for he'd smashed her self-image. Deep inside she'd believed his put-downs, for she had given up her dreams for him, and surely no one with strength and intelligence would have done that!

She'd never actually thought it out, but she'd hung in there, accepting his abuse, doing her dutiful best to be the subservient wife he demanded. She'd known she was turning into a drab little mouse, yet there seemed nothing she could do, and her days had been filled with a gray, monotonous misery.

Until Jason met Rita and walked out on her. Elaine was devastated, convinced she must have failed somehow — that, as Jason claimed, it was all her fault for being so inadequate as a woman —until she slowly realized what a favor Rita had done her. Hard as it had been for a twenty-four-year-old divorcee with a three-year-old daughter (and Jason was no better about paying child support than anything else) to start over, she'd done it.

She'd picked up the dreams she'd put aside for wonderful, manly Jason and gone back after the art degree she'd abandoned for him. She still felt like a mouse, and she de-emphasized her looks as much as possible, but she did it. And if she and Jennifer too often dined on macaroni and cheese, she'd hung on and made ends meet somehow. Along the way, she'd rediscovered things like pride and self-worth, and finally, she'd landed a job with Vaughn and Associates, a fledgling ad agency owned by one Duncan Vaughn.

Duncan was the quiet, non-abrasive sort of man Jason contemptuously categorized as a "wimp," and not even his mother ever accused him of being handsome. His nose was too big, his teeth were crooked, and his hairline was receding...rapidly. He'd also broken his left leg badly as a child and walked with a distinct limp and he was as dark as Jason had been WASP-blond.

But Elaine had nursed a deep bitterness toward all things male. She knew it was wrong —there had to be some decent men — but some of the "friends" who'd offered "help" had been insultingly honest about the "help" they had in mind. So it was good Duncan was so unlike Jason. She'd been wary enough as it was when he offered her the job of art director straight out of school. The money wasn't all that good, but he "sweetened the pot," as he put it, by offering her thirty percent of Vaughn and Associates' stock (which might or might not be valuable someday).

His generosity made her suspicious until she realized that it made hard, practical sense to him because he'd recognized something Jason had never wanted to see in her: Talent. And, unlike Jason, he'd been delighted by it, for he needed her flair for design, and her talent and self—confidence had thrived under the demands he placed upon her.

That was the start. Duncan wrote the copy and handled the clients, Elaine designed and produced the art, and their successes mounted. Slowly at first, but their client list grew steadily, and it was exciting to be doing something, accomplishing something, building something. That was important to them both, and in five years of hard work, they turned Vaughn and Associates into a firm with thirty employees and an annual billing of over three million dollars. Best of all, they did it as a team — as friends and equals who knew perfectly well that neither could have done it without the other.

As time passed, Elaine's wariness of Duncan slowly faded. Her defensiveness eased, and she began discussing non-business things with him, for he was a good listener who offered advice (when he had it) without Jason's Olympian air of stooping to solve some stupid female's silly problems. She felt comfortable with him, yet it never occurred to her that it was any more than friendship between two professionals who respected one another.

But then, after they'd worked together for almost six years without ever really socializing, he unexpectedly asked her to the theater for her birthday and she suddenly had to decide how she really felt about him. She considered very carefully, and her conclusions disturbed her. She certainly didn't feel the bright, jagged, hormonal thing she'd felt for Jason before it turned gray and dreary—but what she did feel was softer and warmer; gentler, with the capacity to do what her feelings for Jason had not — last.

And that worried her. She'd survived a terrible marriage, not without scars, and she was thirty-three-years old, with a daughter who was eleven. Did she want to risk another disaster? Worse, did she want to risk the relationship they had? She doubted their friendship could survive an unsuccessful attempt to make it something more, and she'd seen other successful creative teams crumble when feelings began to cross with business. Nor was her own experience with Jason calculated to make her confident.

Yet when she got that far, she realized Jason's shadow still hung over her like a malignant ghost, and that recognition made her suddenly furious. Damn it, she wasn't the vacuum-minded punching bag Jason had tried to make her! She'd proved that professionally and it was time she did the same with her personal life! It was Duncan she was interested in, and the important point wasn't how Jason had treated her, but how Duncan would.

And when she considered it that way, deliberately comparing them, it wasn't even a contest. All Jason had ever had were looks and physique, and she knew what those were worth. In every quality that really counted, limping, homely, slightly overweight Duncan was so far ahead Jason wasn't even in sight.

So she accepted his invitation and the evening was perfect, from the opening moment at the theater to the post-midnight dinner in the intimate little restaurant. They were friends, but there'd been a warm, gentle undertone — a tenderness — which left no doubt they were about to become more.

Belated happiness put a new sparkle in Elaine's eye, and she laid in a whole new wardrobe as she rediscovered the joys of attractiveness. Not only that, but their working relationship actually improved. There was a new bubble in the creative juices, an awareness that verged on telepathy. They still had disagreements—they'd always had them, where their work was concerned, and sometimes they'd been fiery — but their disputes were purely professional, and Elaine knew how excruciatingly rare it was for two people in love to be able to steer clear of disastrous ego-involvement in arguments.

They quickly became lovers — not without embarrassment on her part. Her love life had been non-existent since Jason and she'd felt oddly timid and inexperienced for the mother of a pre-teen daughter. There was a brief moment when she felt almost agonizingly clumsy, but it passed, and that she realized was because Duncan had understood and been extremely deft. He might not be a handsome man, but someone had certainly taught him things Jason had never known! Of course, Jason wouldn't have bothered to learn them. He'd always been more interested in his pleasure than hers, though she hadn't realized it until Duncan showed her the way things could be.

And yet...and yet, there was a curious hesitation in him, one she couldn't quite pin down but knew was there. She knew he loved her, yet there was a stopping point, a degree of commitment he hesitated to make. Or was it that he hesitated to ask her for one? That was certainly possible, yet she was certain he must know how eager she was to do just that!

But she was no longer shy, mousy little Elaine, so she sent Jennifer to her grandmother's for the Memorial Day weekend and invited Duncan to Friday supper. It was, she acknowledged, sneaky of her, for she hadn't warned him that Jennifer was away, and he was coming under the misapprehension that it would be a family affair — which, she was determined, it most definitely would not be!

Her penniless days were behind her, and she prepared with care. For a man who respected professional women, Duncan was a sucker for ones who looked delicately feminine, and she took unscrupulous advantage of his weakness. Her makeup was sultrier than she ever wore to the office, and her long-sleeved blouse was white silk, delicately embroidered and frilly. A high-waisted skirt of heavy, burgundy velvet clung to her shapely legs, emphasized her tiny waist and swirled intriguingly when she moved. The lingerie under it was her Sunday punch: Her wispy pushup bra puckered her blouse with her uncovered nipples, and she wore smoky-white nylons and a sexy garter belt. Her panties were silk, plunging in front and absurdly tiny, and as a final touch, she purchased a brand new pair of the spike-heeled sandals Duncan loved.

He never had a chance. She smiled at his dropped jaw when she opened the door and her eyes danced as his nostrils flared to the sweet, slightly decadent scent of her perfume. He wore casual denims and a sports shirt, and the contrast between their clothing was perfect. It emphasized her own deliberate preparations and sweet sexiness.

She ushered him into the candlelit dining room, and he sat in a daze. She'd taken tremendous pains over supper, but he scarcely noticed, for his attention was fixed exactly, and flatteringly, where she'd intended — on her.

And then she faced him over the empty plates, sipping wine. Her stereo played softly. Mellow candlelight spilled over her dark hair and glowed in her eyes, and Duncan's face showed exactly the mix of relaxation and desire she'd wanted to create. The moment had come.

"Duncan," she said softly, "you know I love you. Do you love me?" If her question surprised him, he didn't show it.

"More than I ever thought I could love someone," he said simply.

"I'm glad," she said softly, eyes bright with joy, "but if you do — and if you know I love you —why are you holding back?"

He froze, and Elaine caught her breath at the tension which flashed suddenly through him. What in the world could have caused it?

174

This anxious, almost frightened man wasn't her gentle, confident Duncan...yet he was.

"Why," he asked carefully, "do you think I'm holding back?"

"I don't think you are, I know you are. And I don't want you to, Duncan. Whatever's bothering you — worrying you — share it with me, please."

"I don't know if I can," he said finally. "No, I can, I just don't know if I should, because I do love you—God, how I love you! And..." he frowned down into his wine, "I don't want to lose you."

"Lose me?" Elaine stared at him in astonishment. "Unless you're an ax murderer, you're not going to 'lose' me Duncan!"

"Oh?" He smiled crookedly, "not even if I'm interested in bondage?"

For a moment the words didn't register, but then shock hit. Bondage? Her gentle Duncan was into bondage?! That was...it was impossible!

"Bondage?" she said finally, her soft voice just a bit frightened. "You mean like whips and chains?"

"Chains, maybe," he said unhappily, "not whips. And your question's the reason I never told you, Elaine. It scares you, doesn't it?"

She wanted to deny it, but she couldn't and she nodded, gripping her hands together in her lap and staring at him as if he'd become a total stranger.

"I knew it would," he sighed. "God knows the last thing you need after the son-of-a-bitch you married is to feel threatened by a man who says he loves you! I don't want to scare you, and I'd never ask you to do anything you don't want to. I hope you know and believe that."

He met her eyes levelly, and again she nodded. It was odd. She seemed to have become two people — one who recognized her own Duncan, and another who was terrified of the stranger he had become. Yet she was exquisitely, perfectly balanced between her two selves, as if a breath could tip her either way.

"I dropped a few hints that went right by you, so I knew you'd never even thought about it, and I wasn't going to ask you to. But then you asked, and you deserve my honesty.

"Bondage doesn't have to be what the world assumes, Elaine. You asked about whips, and that's what most people seem to think of as soon as they hear the word. They think it can only be an expression of a need to put people down and hurt the other person. That anyone who wants to tie someone up has to be sick and anyone who lets someone tie them up has to want to be hurt.

"That's why I never mentioned it. How could I, after what you've been through? But bondage—my kind of bondage—isn't like that. It's not an excuse to abuse someone. It's...a love game, a fantasy. Something to share. You don't have to be some sort of chauvinistic creep to think women look soft and sexy in bondage, and you don't have to be weak to let someone put you in bondage. What you do have to have is total, mutual trust, and I think that's part of what makes it so special to me.

"But," he held her eyes with the same level gaze, "I watched you put yourself back together after that bastard. You never said much about it, but I know he was more than just verbally abusive, and I would never— never—do anything to hurt or diminish you. So I decided I'd never even ask you to try it, because I can live without it, Elaine. I enjoy bondage, I don't need it, and I do need you. But when you asked...well..." he smiled a sad little smile, "one thing I can't do is lie to you, especially not when that could hurt so much if you found out later and didn't understand why I had."

"But you would like to tie me up, wouldn't you?" Elaine asked softly, eyes huge in the candlelight, and he nodded slowly.

"I would. I do — but I can live without it. I won't pretend there won't be any regrets, but I've already decided I can handle those, and I'll never pressure you about it."

Elaine knew she was breathing hard, and sweat prickled in her shaven armpits. He meant it. Every word of it. He wanted to tie her up, and he'd really intended to never even ask her. He knew what she'd been through, how the thought of restraint must frighten her, and he'd refused to frighten her. She could tell it was more important to him than he wanted her to think, yet she was more important still. And despite her shock—despite a feeling that the world had turned to quicksand—that touched her. Jason would never have admitted his desires unless he meant to hound her into submitting to them; Duncan had admitted them, knowing they might turn her away, and he had no intention of pushing her at all. And that, she thought, was the true difference between them.

She rose wordlessly, mind whirring, and gathered the dishes. She carried them into the kitchen, feeling his tension behind her as she left the dining room but she couldn't speak. She had to think. She had to understand. How could it be the way he said? To tie someone up had to be a putdown, didn't it? And she knew how cruelly she could be hurt and humiliated by someone she thought she loved. Wouldn't tying her be a way of saying she was less important than he was? That Duncan held the power — the authority — in their relationship? And could she renounce her hard-won freedom, submit to being tied, without diminishing herself?

She didn't know, and she wondered how she would have reacted if he'd asked her months ago. What if he'd told her what he wanted at the very start? She paused, a plate poised over the dishwasher, astounded to discover that she had absolutely no idea! On the one hand, the idea frightened her with its echo of Jason; on the other, the suggestion would have come from Duncan. Sweet, gentle Duncan, the one man she truly, completely trusted. Would she have agreed? Would she have tried it to please him? And if she had, how would she have felt? How would she have reacted? Responded?

She didn't know, yet there was a strange tingle within her. One mixed up with her anxiety and shock, but neither anxious nor shocked. It was a quivery shiver, and it glowed with sensuality. To be tied, she thought. To be bound, utterly in Duncan's power. To make love that way...What would that do to her? To know she'd surrendered herself to him totally, however temporarily? Trust. That was what if came down to, wasn't it?

Trust...and the knowledge that she loved him and he loved her.

She put the plate in the dishwasher, squared her shoulders and opened a drawer, and her breathing was just a bit harder than usual. Duncan looked up as she returned and she saw it all in his eyes—desire for her, awareness of her loveliness — and fear that he'd frightened her away forever.

"You say you want to tie me up," she said softly, "and you're right —I would have to trust you. But you have to understand, Duncan, it's more than just trust. I...it scares me, because you're right about how far back I had to come after Jason. But then, you helped me do that, didn't you?"

"You would've done it without me," he said gently.

"I didn't say you did it for me; I said you helped. You did, and I do love you...and trust you. And I think..." she drew a breath and brought her hand in front of her, showing him the shrink wrapped cotton clothes-line from the drawer "that we'd better find out how I feel about bondage."

She watched his face, and his joy reached out to her like a caress. She saw his delighted, erotic eagerness to bind her — but there was gentleness behind the delight. A tenderness that recognized how much her offer cost her and he loved her for her courage. Yet he sat motionless and spoke softly.

"Are you positive, Elaine? I'd be lying to say I don't want to do it, but are you sure you want to try it?"

"Want to?" Her ripe lips trembled slightly. "No, I'm not sure I want to, but I need to. I have to know Duncan, and I want to trust you and show us both how much I do. Does that make sense?"

"It does to me," he said quietly. He rose, holding out his hand, and she surrendered the clothesline almost timidly. Her muscles quivered with shuddery uncertainty and her breath came quick and fluttery, but her anxiety mingled with her other feelings and a bright tide of sensitivity and sensuality seemed to be pouring through her veins.

Crinkling plastic rattled as he opened the package, and she stared at the smooth, white rope. Five minutes ago, it had been everyday ordinary cord; a friendly household servant, convenient for its utility and totally unthreatening. Now it had changed. It had become the tool of her surrender, a braided emblem of trust and a frightening magic wand to turn her whole world topsy-turvy.

He uncoiled the cord, smoothing the kinks between his fingers, then laid it on the table and turned to her. He opened his arms and she burrowed into them, clinging to him desperately. She'd never done anything like this — never even considered it — and she felt frightened and a little bit wicked, all at the same time. This was forbidden, taboo, and exciting, and she began to tremble as he unbuttoned the back of her blouse. It was far from the first time he'd undressed her. He loved to peel her garments slowly and teasingly, drawing out the moments of her revelation, and she loved for him to do it.

But tonight was different. Tonight he was going to tie her up, and that made everything new and fiery and anxious. The blouse opened and she clung to him like a reluctant child, releasing her hold only when his gentle hands insisted. She stood before him, staring at his shoes, unable to meet his eyes as he eased the silk down her arms, and she felt his eyes —smoky with desire—on her naked nipples. Nipples, she realized with a blush, as high and hard as they'd ever been in her life!

She closed her eyes and savored the strange sensations rippling through her as he unhooked her skirt. Her skin shuddered with cat-footed shivers, as if someone were scrubbing his nails over a blackboard, yet a hot, liquid heat pulsed deep within her. She felt it in her womb, damp and urgent between her smooth thighs, and a slow, sensual moan trembled through her as her skirt fell about her feet in a heavy, wine-colored puddle.

"God, you're beautiful," he whispered, and she bit her lip against a startled cry as he caressed her bare ribs and fluttering belly. His touch was so unexpected it shocked her, but that was part of the magic. She had no guide, no warning of what would happen, yet her uncertainty wasn't the cold, scary thing it would have been with Jason. This panting ignorance — this singing, exciting tension — was bright-edged lightning in her nerves.

His hands were so gentle, so utterly familiar...and so totally strange! They belonged to a stranger, she thought, shuddering as they stroked her firm bottom and the backs of her thighs, a stranger who knew her intimately. Someone who knew her every secret, her every sensitivity. His touch was fiery above her nylons, and she opened her legs, spreading them to offer him their softness.

Moth-wing fingers caressed the satin of her inner thighs, and her hips spasmed at the sudden fire in her belly and blood. But then those gentle hands gathered her wrists before her, and she wanted to look into his eyes, but she couldn't. She just couldn't. She could only stare at their hands—her own limp and trusting, his a stranger's—as he crossed her delicate wrists and reached for the rope.

Thin cord looped and tightened, and her eyes widened. Her hips rolled and breath hissed in her flared nostrils. If felt so strange! It was too snug to slip, impossible to escape, yet gentle — constricting but not hurting. It embodied a subtle paradox of tenderness and compulsion that perfected one another in some mysterious way she understood no more than she understood the silken fire in her veins.

And then he knotted the cord, and her bound hands fell, too weak to resist gravity. She gasped as they brushed her pelvis, and blushed as she smelled her own passion. The fingers of one hand curled of their own volition, half-shielded by their restrained companion as they stroked her molten core through her panties, and a spike of fire roared within her.

She raised her eyes at last, and they were wide and soft, appealing to him for instruction while she squeezed her own wet softness through her sodden panties. She'd never done anything like that in her life. Never stood before husband or lover and caressed herself, yet now she couldn't stop herself! It wasn't a compulsion. No one had asked her to. It was just...inevitable, and as natural as breathing.

He kissed her, and his tongue snaked into her mouth ruthlessly — like a man claiming his treasure as his own — yet it was a shared ruthlessness; breathless, but not frightening, and her liquid tongue met his ardently, inviting it deeper as she moaned against his mouth, pressing her breasts against his sports shirt and squeezing herself harder than ever.

She'd never felt such wonderful hunger and fulminating need! That small edge of fear still touched her, but somehow it only made the moment even more perfect, and she whimpered when he broke the kiss at last.

"Not yet," he whispered, licking the tip of her nose, and stepped back, tugging on her wrist rope. She followed with hip-shot grace, and her eyes were a fiery glory. She preened, feeling his desire as if their minds were linked, and moved with a sultry grace as he drew her back to the table and picked up his wineglass.

He raised it wordlessly to her lips, holding her bound hands down with their tether, and she drank thirstily. Wine had never tasted so sweet, and she knew it was the way it was offered—the way he held the glass when she could not — which made it so. A ruby drop splashed her breasts and trickled down her cleavage, and its cool, wet kiss was yet another lover's caress.

"Now," he murmured, and set the glass aside. He gripped her shoulders gently, urging her backward, and she went eagerly, all hesitation lost. She'd strayed through Alice's looking glass, and her familiar dining room was a place of exotic mystery, filled with the erotic secret which Duncan was about to teach her.

The table pressed her bottom, and she whimpered as he eased her back. She lay across the white tablecloth, bound hands rising to her breasts in an instinctive pretense of modesty, and he smiled. "None of that now!" he teased, circling the table with her tether. "Give me your hands, Elaine," he commanded softly, and she gasped as he pulled.

Her hands rose, as obedient to his command as to his cord, and she closed her eyes once more, belly fluttering, hips jerking to a drum roll flicker of fire as he stole her arms. They framed her face, and the cord trembled as he tied it. Then it was done, her arms were bound above her head, pinning her to her own table, and he circled back to her feet. He knelt, and she raised her head slowly, opening her eyes with carnal languor, and blushed.

She could see only his eyes over her pelvis — eyes, inches from the wet, silk-covered swell of her mound. She knew he saw the tendrils of passion leaking from her panties, for she felt them on her smoking skin and smelled them...as he did, she thought. But then the rope bit her left ankle, as gently, implacably tight as the cords on her wrists, and her head fell back, rolling in the triangle of her arms. She whimpered as he lashed her small foot to the top of a table leg, cording it back and to the side, lifting her toes from the floor and parting her thighs, and then he began to tie her other foot!

She held her breath, shuddering, eyes closed, and it was done. She was bound to the table, exposed, a fragile sacrifice to his passion, and she'd never felt so delicately, desirably female in her entire life. He'd done it, she thought wonderingly. He'd tied her up, and there was no more fear. There was only this exultant glory and sense of her own beauty; the knowledge that she could surrender to him, trust him. And joy and discovery banished Jason's ghost at last. Its cold, selfish cruelty could not live in the bright light of Duncan's tenderness.

"There," he said softly. "You're bound—but not entirely. Do you want it to be perfect, Elaine? Do you want to be bound completely?"

"Yes," she whispered hoarsely, blushing at her own eagerness. "Yes!"

"Then open your mouth," he murmured, and she heard the rustle of cloth as he balled a linen napkin tightly. She moaned, but her mouth opened wide, and she strained her jaws to admit it as he packed it tenderly inside.

So strange, she thought moltenly. So strange! She whimpered — a soft, eager, cloth-clogged sound — as a gentle hand raised her head and he looped another napkin around her mouth. He knotted it tight, stretching the corners of her mouth with just a hint of ruthlessness, and she closed her eyes. She was bound, unable to move, and gagged, unable to speak. Escape was impossible.

She couldn't even protest! She'd yielded herself into his hands, and if her bondage was of her own choosing, it was also real. She'd made herself as acutely vulnerable as a woman could be, and that smoked through her like a fire cloud and danced on her skin like ozone.

Yet she felt no fear. Anxiety, yes — but it was a bright thing — a breathless awareness that she stood on the cusp of the new and wonderful, for this was Duncan, her Duncan. He had the power to do whatever he wished with and to her, but he would never, could never, hurt her. She knew that, knew it beyond the shadow of a doubt, and in that moment she understood exactly what he'd meant about trust. The total, uncompromising faith in his fidelity which let her put herself at risk and prove their love to them both.

She opened her eyes slowly, staring up, slender and powerless in his ropes, and shuddered at his expression. His eyes glowed, and she swallowed behind her silence-swollen mouth as she realized she wasn't powerless at all. She was imbued with the magic power of her love and her courage to yield. Her trust was stronger than any chain, inescapable as any rope, making him hers as she had made herself his, and bondage diminished neither of them, for there was no question of superiority and inferiority, but only her gift—her gift of herself—freely given and gently accepted.

He smiled and went slowly back to his knees, and she stared up at the ceiling, trembling and taut in the stretchy mastery of his cords. His fingers hooked into her panties, easing them down, and she whimpered as he bared her silken wedge and swollen petals. She knew they were wet, delicately unfurled, beckoning to him, and she groaned as hot breath flowed over them.

Her bound hands clenched in fists, and her spine arched as his mouth touched. She moaned, then sobbed, then squealed under the merciless magic of his lips. She wailed, thrusting against him, joyously shameless. She became his silk-skinned wanton, without hesitation or reserve, and wept as the soft, liquid sounds of his mouth filled her universe and stoked the roaring furnace within her. She smoked and fumed, wailing and alive, trembling on the lip of eruption.

And then he stopped. Stopped instantly, without warning, and she sobbed, the sound a hacking groan of gagged protest. She rolled her hips blatantly, frantic to entice his mouth back, and he laughed softly. So softly! There was no mockery in it, only an endless, loving, teasing tenderness.

Then the ice bucket clinked and something gurgled. She raised her head, her brown eyes wild and fiery with need, and wailed in protest as she saw him pouring wine. He only smiled — and then nested the cold, wet bottle into her lowered panties! The silk held its chill, slick glass against her molten loins, and she squealed in shock as he sipped.

"Not yet, sweetheart," he whispered as he lowered the glass. She moaned pleadingly, hips squirming, gasping as the cold bottle caressed her like a deliciously perverse lover, and he tickled her deep, fluttering navel.

"You'll just have to wait, won't you, you hot little darling?" he teased, and she sobbed with imploring hot-eyed acceptance. "I'll make you come...eventually, but waiting's part of the game, Elaine—part of being mine." He reached out and turned the bottle slowly, smiling as she groaned and pressed her hot, clinging wetness to the chill glass.

"I'll just finish this glass," he said lovingly, "and then I'll play with you some more. A lot more. And when you're ready to come..." her eyes brightened as he paused tantalizingly, "I'll stop for another glass." She sobbed, rolling her head. It was awful! Terrible!! She was dying, burning to windblown ash in the furnace he'd lit within her, and he wouldn't do anything about it! No, that wasn't right —he was going to make it worse...and so much better!

He took another sip — a longer one, emptying the glass — and her eyes glowed as he removed the bottle gently. He went back to his knees, and the soft breath of his laughter flowed over her fevered flesh. "You know," he teased, "that bottle's almost full. It'll take quite a few glasses to empty it, won't it?" His tongue darted wickedly, and she squealed in frantic, hungry delight. Then he pulled back. "Poor baby, you'll probably be right out of your mind before it's all gone, won't you?" She writhed urgently, her eyes afire with the wonder and delight of her bondage, and he leaned forward to kiss her belly.

"Glad you tried it?" he whispered, and her loving croon and frantic nod answered. "Good. Because this is going to take all night, I think, and then there's the weekend." She moaned in delight, and he laughed, but then he spoke again, his soft voice infinitely tender.

"You've given me something I would never have dared ask for, Elaine, and I love you. I love you so much!" Then he grinned impishly, banishing his sudden tenderness, and his eyes glinted with deviltry. "But just because you're brave, beautiful and wonderful doesn't mean I'll show you any mercy! I expect you'll carry on quite a bit, like this..." his darting tongue wrung a joyous wail from his pulsing girlfriend, "before we get to the happy ending. But we'll get there, Elaine, I promise, and then..." he licked her again, and her frantic squeal was shrill and jubilant, "we'll live happily ever after."

He bent back to his loving task, and Elaine's world dissolved into bright, pulsating glory.

SHARON'S TALE

Sharon closed her car door and walked along the stone walkway to her front door. Already the work week was fading. It was Friday, and all that lay ahead of her now was a weekend of rest. She certainly would've preferred that Mark hadn't run off golfing for the entire weekend without her, but she didn't want to think about that now.

Sharon stopped thinking about Mark and looked down by the front door. On the porch lay a small package about the size of a shoe box. It was wrapped in plain brown paper and had been hand delivered, for there was no address on the package, only a note that was taped to the outside.

She picked up the package and went inside, reading the note as she walked:

"Dearest Sharon,

I've just found the most wonderful store. I went crazy. I got these for you. Mark will love them.

Call me. Vanessa."

How strange. She hadn't talked to Vanessa for ages. It was as if her best friend had walked off the face of the earth. For two months, Sharon couldn't find her, then suddenly, out of the blue, this.

Sharon ripped open the package to reveal a shoe box. Thinking that Vanessa packed something else in the shoe box, Sharon was surprised to find an incredibly beautiful pair of black stiletto pumps inside. She had never received a pair of shoes as a gift from a girlfriend before. Well, certainly not like these, anyway.

Vanessa took one of the shoes out of the box and examined it. It was her size — 6b. It was imported from Italy and made of patent leather. The tapered heel was very thin, and had to be more than 5 inches high. Connected to the top of each shoe were thin ankle straps.

These shoes must have cost a fortune, she thought, as she sat down on the sofa and kicked off her work shoes, eager to try them on. She slid the shoes onto her stockinged feet and found that they did, indeed, fit perfectly. She took a quick look at the ankle straps. They didn't buckle together as she first thought. The end of one strap clipped into a receptacle at the end of the other strap. Strange, she thought, as she attached the straps together with a barely discernible click. She admired the shoes for a short time, and then carefully stood up and walked over to the full length mirror to get a better look.

Wow! she said aloud, as she lifted her skirt and looked at the line of her leg. She bent over, and slid her hands up her soft stockings, admiring the way the high heels made her legs look longer. Sharon knew she had great legs, but these shoes made them look even better. Maybe if I wore something like this, Jack wouldn't be so eager to run off with his buddies, she thought. How dreary this house was without him.

The golf trip had been planned for weeks, but Mark knew Sharon was unhappy with him. She would have much preferred it if he had stayed home and made passionate love to her all weekend, like he used to do. Sharon began to wonder if the spark had gone out of their marriage. The second she thought it, she wished she hadn't, and tried to put it out of her mind; but it was too late, it had already depressed her.

She walked back over to the sofa and sat down. She bent over to take off the shoes and stopped. She couldn't find a release for the ankle strap. She felt around the closure for a release, but there was none. Frustrated, she lifted her foot and looked at the closure. On the side of the closure was a tiny keyhole. She grabbed the shoe box and looked inside. No key. She tried pulling on the straps to see if they would just release, but they were solidly attached to one another. How am I going to get these shoes off without ruining them? she thought, already picking up the phone to call Vanessa.

"Hello?"

"Vanessa, its Sharon. I got the shoes."

"Aren't they great?!" Vanessa said.

"They're beautiful..." Sharon said, feeling a little silly, "but... well.. I tried them on, and now I can't take them off... They're kind of locked on. I think they need a key and it isn't in the box. Please tell me you have it."

"Hold on," Vanessa said, putting down the phone. "It's here. I'm so sorry. Somehow they key didn't get in the box. Hey, isn't Jack golfing this weekend?"

"Yes. How did you know?"

"Well, Tim's out of town for the weekend too. Why don't you drive down here for dinner tonight. I know it's a long way, but you can stay the night if you like. We'll have time to talk. There are so many things that have happened to me over the last few months. I must see you. I might even consider releasing you from your shoes, if you ask me nicely." It didn't take Sharon long to decide, "That sounds great. Let's do it. I've just got to pack a few things and I'll be there... Bye."

Sharon put down the phone and walked into the bedroom. She hadn't wanted to stay in the house tonight by herself anyway. She stepped out of her dress, being very careful not to rip it with her stiletto shoes, and hung it up in the closet. Because she couldn't take her incredibly sexy shoes off, she decided she would go all out and wear her black mini outfit. She grabbed it and put it on. The dress barely covered the dark tops of her black stockings. "Jack, you don't know what you're missing," she said aloud, as she quickly packed some clothes in an overnight bag and left.

Traffic was good, and it only took an hour and a half to drive the ninety- five miles to Woodcrest. Vanessa lived in a large house, on a fairly good sized lot. It was quiet and secluded. Just the type of weekend I needed, she thought as she drove up the long driveway to the house. She climbed out of her car, grabbed her bag and walked up to the door. It opened before she got there. Sharon stopped dead in her tracks.

In the doorway, Vanessa stood in one of the most erotic outfits Sharon had ever seen. Vanessa was wearing a black and red turtle-neck teddy that was cut high on the hips to accentuate Vanessa's beautiful legs. The teddy was made out of some kind of patent material that was so tight and shiny that it looked like someone had just poured it on her body, and it was still wet. To complement her teddy, she had put on a pair of long, jet black stockings and a pair of black patent leather ankle boots with 5-inch stiletto heels. The tops of the boots weren't tight around her legs; they flared out a bit, in- tensifying the line of her slender ankles. Sharon didn't move. She just stood there staring.

"Isn't it great?!" Vanessa said beaming.

"Impressive," Sharon said, collecting herself. "Where on earth did you pick up that?"

"On my trip to Europe. There was this great shop called 'Dress for Duress'. I couldn't be- lieve it. I bought a ton of stuff. Come on in."

"What brought this on?"

Sharon asked completely dumbfounded. "It's Jim's fault, really. It started innocently enough. Sit down...would you like some wine?"

"Sure. What started innocently?" Sharon said, watching Vanessa as she strutted to the bar. Sharon was completely overwhelmed. She couldn't take her eyes off of Vanessa's incredibly sexy body as her friend poured two glasses of wine and brought them back to the couch.

"Here," Vanessa said, handing Sharon a glass of wine. "I don't know where to begin. I guess at the beginning. One day, I was innocently cleaning one of Jim's cabinets, when I found a bondage magazine."

"Bondage?! What? Like, whips and chains?"

"No, not exactly. Just women dressed in all kinds of bizarre outfits, tied up in these amazingly intricate positions. It was actually incredibly erotic.

"Well anyway, when he got home, I confronted him and he came clean. He said he had been into bondage his whole life. I asked him if he had tied up his other girlfriends and he said he had. Then I asked why he hadn't asked to tie me up. He said that he was scared that I wouldn't understand. He said that I was very special to him and that he didn't want to lose me. He had been waiting for the right time to bring it up, but it just had never seemed like the right time.

"Anyway, to make a long story short, we had a long talk about it that night. Then one thing led to another and there I was—tied spread-eagled on the bed."

"Wow. How was it?" Sharon was genuinely intrigued.

"I was a little scared at first, but he was very gentle and soon I was totally into it. It was incredible. He started kissing me all over my body. I was totally turned on. Not being able to get free released my inhibitions and intensified my senses. I was writhing around and making a lot of noise. He grabbed a scarf and gagged me with it, explaining that if I needed to get free, I need only hum a song and he would release me."

"He gagged you? How was that?"

"It was weird, but the gag made me feel even more excited. He took out a vibrator and began to play with me. He was very clever with it. It wasn't more than a couple of minutes before I came. It was the most incredible orgasm I've ever had. After it was over I relaxed, exhausted on the bed, and waiting for him to untie me, but he didn't. He told me that I was going to have to come five times before he would let me go."

"FIVE more times?"

"Yes, It was unbelievable. He had me tied up for over three hours. He had incredible patience. Each orgasm was its own unique act. It was amazing."

"What happened then?"

"After my fifth orgasm, he untied me and I fell into his arms. It was weird. I had never felt so loved in all my life. Ever since then, things have kind of evolved."

"Evolved?" Sharon asked, unable to hide the fact that she was hanging on every word.

"Come on, follow me and I'll show you."

Sharon noticed that her panties were wet. She was completely turned on. She gulped down the rest of her wine and followed Vanessa into one of the bedrooms. On the bed was a vast selection of erotic lingerie, all of which tended towards the kinky side. There were various pairs of shoes and boots, all with incredible high heels. Beside the clothing, there was a bunch of rope, handcuffs, and various bondage paraphernalia. She couldn't begin to understand how some of them might be used.

"Oh my God — this is incredible!" Sharon exclaimed.

"This is only a sample. Care to try something on?"

She should have seen it coming, but Sharon was completely un-prepared for the question. She turned, looked at Vanessa, started to say something and then stopped. She waited for Vanessa to say something else, but her friend let the question stand. She thought about it for a minute.

"That's a loaded question," Sharon finally replied. "Did you mean try on one of the outfits, or try out the bondage stuff?"

"Both," Vanessa said, smiling.

Then something strange happened. Even though it was contrary to how she thought she might reply, Sharon heard herself say, "Okay." She wasn't sure why. Something in Vanessa's quiet confidence had taken Sharon completely by surprise. Maybe it was because she was still angry over Mark going off and leaving her. Or maybe she was just totally in-trigued by the whole thing. All she really knew was that her best friend, another woman, had asked her if she wanted to try out a little bondage and she had agreed.

"Let's select an outfit for you. Bondage just isn't bondage without the right packaging," said Vanessa as she grabbed a jet black body stock-ing from the bed and gave it to Sharon. "Here put this on to start with."

"I need the key," Sharon said, looking down at her feet, which were still locked in her shoes.

"Oh sorry, I forgot. Allow me."

Vanessa pulled out the key from a drawer and unlocked the straps around Sharon's ankles. Sharon was grateful and Vanessa removed the shoes from her feet. They had been locked in those shoes for hours, and her feet were sore. Sharon shed her clothes and slid on the long body stocking. It was made of an incredibly soft sheer nylon, and covered her entire body; all the way from her neck to her feet. Vanessa helped her by zipping up the small zipper in the back. Sharon turned and faced

Vanessa.

"That looks great on you," Vanessa said. "Turn around."

Vanessa proceeded to lace her into a shiny black corset that went from the bottom of her breasts to her hips. It was heavily boned and as Vanessa pulled the laces taut, it pushed in on her, making her waist at least three inches smaller.

"God, this is tight. I can barely breath," Sharon complained.

"It's supposed to be — here, " Vanessa gave Sharon a pair of long black PVC gloves. Sliding her arms into them, Sharon discovered that the gloves fit like a second skin, and went way up past her elbows. "Now some shoes. These will do. Put them on." Vanessa handed Sharon a pair of 5 inch, black stiletto pumps. They were very similar to the pair that she had been imprisoned in, but without the straps. "Oh... Do I have to? I just got those other shoes off my feet," complained Sharon. Vanessa just stared at her and it became clear that the shoes were required.

Sharon obediently sat down and put the shoes on. Then she carefully stood up and walked over to the mirror. She looked unbelievable. She turned around and looked at herself. She felt powerful and feminine all at the same time. "You look stunning!" Vanessa said walking up from behind. "Just one final touch." She brushed Sharon's shoulder length blond hair and tied it up with a black ribbon, making a big, black bow on the back of Sharon's head.

"Perfect, Gwendoline would have been proud."

"Gwendoline who?" Sharon asked.

"I'll explain later. Come with me." Sharon did as she was told, and followed Vanessa over to the bed. "Turn around, and put your hands behind your back." Sharon turned around and slowly did as she was bid. Now that the moment of truth was here, she was a little scared. Even though she trusted Vanessa, she wasn't sure what she was getting into.

"Okay, before we begin, I just want you to know that we can stop anytime you want. Just hum a tune, any tune, and I'll untie you immediately. Okay? Do you want to continue?"

"Yes," Sharon replied, acknowledging within herself that she did. She was already incredibly turned on. This was all so new and exciting. She didn't want to stop now.

"Okay, put your hands together, palm to palm," Vanessa directed. Sharon obeyed, and Vanessa took a length of rope and wrapped it around her friend's gloved wrists.

She wrapped loosely at first, but then as she cinched the ropes between the wrists, it tightened evenly, securely binding Sharon's hands. Then, Vanessa took another length of rope and began to wrap it around Sharon's upper arms, just above the elbows. As she tightened the ropes, it pulled Sharon's elbows back until they were nearly touching behind her. Vanessa expertly cinched and tied off the ropes. "I knew you were limber," Vanessa said.

"Is it really necessary for it to be this tight?" Sharon asked, struggling experimentally.

"Absolutely. I can't have you getting free on me, can I?"

Sharon continued to test her bonds. After a short time, it was obvious that there was indeed no way she was going to get free without Vanessa's help.

"How do you feel?" Vanessa asked.

"Very restrained. I can't possibly get free... You can do anything you want to me."

"I know," Vanessa said as she doubled a length of rope and looped it around Sharon's corseted waist a few times. Sharon wondered what she was doing, until Vanessa fed the ends of the rope through the loop and pulled it between her legs.

"What are you doing to me?" Sharon murmured as Vanessa carefully placed the crotch-rope, centering and adjusting the rope before she pulled it taut. "This is called a crotch-rope," Vanessa said, yanking on the rope. "Delicious isn't it?"

"Oooo..."

Vanessa attached the rope to Sharon's waist ropes, making sure that the crotch-rope was tight against Sharon's flesh. Tying the crotch-rope to her hands allowed Sharon a little fun. She soon found that every time she moved her hands the rope between her legs would tighten, sending waves of pleasure through her body.

"That's right, struggle," Vanessa said quietly as she reached around and cupped Sharon's breasts in her hands. "Struggle all you want, you can't get free. You're mine now."

"Oh yes.." Sharon whispered as Vanessa's hand slid down her body and between her legs. Vanessa slowly caressed Sharon's sex with one hand while the other grabbed the crotch-rope and pulled it tighter, forcing it and the nylon body stocking even further inside Sharon's body. Vanessa continued to play with Sharon, expertly alternating between soft and rough caresses, until she had brought Sharon to the very brink of orgasm. Then she stopped.

"Oh, please don't stop... Please?" cried Sharon.

"I think it's time for some more ropes," said Vanessa, in response to Sharon's impassioned plea.

"No, please, don't stop... Not now," Sharon whimpered.

"I think it's also time for you to be quiet," Vanessa said as she grabbed a red ball gag. "Remember, if something isn't right, or you really feel the need to get free, just hum a tune, any tune. Okay?"

"Okay."

"Now, open your mouth. Wider." Vanessa slowly worked the ball-gag into Sharon's mouth, until Sharon felt the red orb pop in behind her teeth. The gag filled her mouth and tasted strange. Vanessa buckled it tightly behind her head, turned and began to remove all the extra stuff from the bed. Meanwhile, Sharon tested the efficiency of the ball-gag. She tried unsuccessfully to push it out of her mouth with her tongue, but it was inside her mouth to stay. With the gag so firmly strapped in place, Sharon felt even more attracted now to the concept that she couldn't stop Vanessa from whatever she might do.

Vanessa returned and led Sharon to the bed, but instead of having her lie down, she had her kneel on it, facing the foot of the bed. Vanessa took a black bar about one and a half feet in length and tied Sharon's knees to both ends of it. Then she crossed Sharon's ankles behind her and tied them together.

Another rope was added attaching her ankles to the head of the bed. Then Vanessa took a long length of rope, attached it to Sharon's elbow ropes, and looped it tightly around her torso, above and below her breasts, tying it off behind the back. Next, she took a piece of rope, attached one end to Sharon's elbow rope and the other end to the head board, pulling it tight. Three more ropes were added; one was attached from Sharon's waist rope to the foot of the bed in front of her, and two others on either side of her.

As Vanessa tightened the rope in front, Sharon's body was pulled forward until she was unable to sit down on her feet. The ropes on either side made it impossible to fall sideways. Vanessa stepped back and admired her handiwork. Sharon was admiring it as well. Not only could she barely move — Vanessa had made it impossible for her to sit down. The ropes held her firmly upright. All she could do was slowly squirm in place.

"Oh, you look superb. Let me show you," cooed Vanessa, and she positioned some small spot lights around Sharon and then turned off all the other lights in the room. She went away, and then quickly came back with a set of large mirrors, which she proceeded to set up around the bed. When she was finished, Sharon had no choice but to look at herself from every angle. She couldn't believe how sexy she looked. There were ropes everywhere.

She watched herself as she slowly struggled against them. Various fantasies crept into her mind. She was a damsel in distress, awaiting some cruel fate, or on the auction block. The list was endless. Vanessa had disappeared and left Sharon alone to struggle and contemplate her bondage. The loneliness intensified the experience even more. She watched herself intently. Focusing on her body and the flex of the rope as she continued to struggle, she knew that escape was impossible.

After a few minutes, Vanessa returned from the dark portion of the room. She had been watching Sharon's excitement build and she felt it was time. She had removed most of her outfit (except for her stockings) and had put on some long black satin gloves.

"How's my beauty?" Vanessa asked, as she climbed on the bed. Her gloved hands slowly moved over her friend's writhing body, until she reached Sharon's crotch.

"Oh, you're so wet. Look how wet your sex is."

"Mmmm," Sharon moaned into her gag, trying to twist away, unable to resist. Vanessa stopped her caresses and went around behind Sharon. She took off Sharon's shoes and placed them on the floor. "Isn't that better?" she asked, as she began to rub and massage Sharon's stockinged feet. She bent over and began to suck Sharon's stockinged toes, kissing and licking the soles and heels of Sharon's feet, moving slowly up the stocking-covered legs, and on up to her friend's torso and breasts. Vanessa paused at Sharon's neck and ears, then went down her friend's body again, always passing by the one area that Sharon longed for her to kiss. Vanessa repeated this innumerable times, taking particular pleasure in the tension that she was building in Sharon's bound body.

After she felt that Sharon had had enough, she finally relented and concentrated on Sharon's aching nether region. Sharon soon discovered that Vanessa had an expert tongue, and seemed to know instinctively just when to kiss or tickle, and suck or bite. Soon, Sharon was writhing around in utter ecstasy; straining at the bonds that held her firmly in place. When Vanessa felt Sharon was ready, she pulled out a small vibrator and began to massage Sharon's crotch through the crotch-rope. This made Sharon go crazy, moaning and struggling, not to get free, but to reach climax. Vanessa concentrated on Sharon's reactions. She watched the tension build. Her friend's hands gripped the crotch-rope, stockinged feet arching, eyes shut tight. Sharon was straining for release.

Vanessa waited patiently until Sharon was just about to come, then pulled the vibrator away, leaving it just a half inch away from her friend's crotch. Sharon opened her eyes and looked down at Vanessa, who was smiling broadly and slowly moving the head of the vibrator back and forth, teasingly.

She tried to lower herself down on the vibrator, but found (to her dismay) that the ropes prevented her from touching it. She struggled harder, trying in vain to reach the vibrator, so she could relieve the incredible longing that Vanessa had built up inside her.

"Struggle for me Sharon. That's right. Do you want it?" Vanessa asked, lightly touching Sharon's sex with the vibrator, then pulling it away again.

"Okay, you deserve it," Vanessa said and pulled it tighter, forcing it and the nylon body stocking even further inside Sharon's body.

"Mmmm," Sharon moaned into her gag, trying to twist away, unable to resist.

"Mmph..." Sharon whimpered through her gag as she continued to struggle against the cunning ropes in order to lower herself onto the vibrator.

"Oooo, you do want it, don't you?" teased Vanessa, again lightly touching Sharon's crotch, and again, immediately taking it away.

"MMMPH!" Sharon screamed into her gag in frustration.

"Okay, you've earned it," Vanessa said as she pushed the head of the vibrator hard against the ropes that shielded Sharon's intimate treasures. Almost immediately, Sharon came. She shuddered as waves of pleasure washed over her, again and again. She came longer than she ever had before, and then collapsed, the ropes still holding her limp body firmly upright.

Vanessa removed the vibrator and kissed Sharon's gagged lips. Sharon looked into Vanessa's eyes, silently wondering if she was going to be released. Vanessa seemed to read her thoughts. "Oh no, my sweet playmate, this was just an overture to your evening of pleasure!" With that, Vanessa got out a blindfold and put it over Sharon's eyes. Sharon couldn't believe it. Vanessa was going to do all of that to her again?!

Sharon waited in anticipation for the pleasure to begin again, but instead she heard Vanessa's stockinged legs rustle on the bedspread as she slid off the bed and slipped away.

All was darkness. She was alone. Thoughts raced through Sharon's mind about what Vanessa might be doing. What Vanessa had planned next. She strained to listen for her friend's return.

Nothing... Then footsteps! DIFFERENT footsteps!

"Hello, Sharon."

"Mmmmph! " Sharon shouted into her gag as she realized it was Mark.

"Yes, it's me. I have been watching for over an hour. Vanessa set this whole thing up for us," Mark said, as he unbuckled the strap from behind Sharon's head, and pulled the ball-gag from her lips. "I'm here for the entire weekend. Just for you," he said.

"Oh, Mark. Kiss me..."

•

Q&A WITH BONDAGE SUPERMODEL KELLY ASHTON

IN WHOM PHYSICALITY AND INTELLECT GRACIOUSLY CONVERGE

SHE MIGHT BE REASON ENOUGH TO RETHINK THE WONDERS OF THE WORLD!

This one you really oughta see in person. To put it in inelegant street parlance, we're talking serious major babe here.

Kelly Ashton is likely one of the most physically striking females any of us will ever get to see. Once you've regarded her fabulous face and heart-stopping figure, you realize the one and only thing this woman can never be is unnoticed. Not many women are taller. Hardly any at all are as tall all over. And we wager that nary a one who is that tall - six feet or so - possesses such a strikingly-rounded body—chest, waistline and hips to ignite a lifetime of fairly shameful fantasies.

It's as though Nature disputed some guy's version of a great-looking woman by whipping up Kelly Ashton and then pointing to one and then the other and saying, "Nah, that's no great-looking woman...*this* is a great-looking woman!" And to this truly magnificent fantasy woman, Nature considerately added intellect and a genuine heartbeat.

Kelly is educated and bright—

within sighting distance of a PHD in psychology. She is one very evolved human being. Best of all, she is sincere. Some of the things she has to say about bondage would seem too good to be true. But her answers came after our request that she not tell us what she thought we might want to hear—that she speak her absolute truth, no matter how disappointing to us that might be. To us, and we hope to you, she is completely convincing about her feelings regarding bondage and people who are drawn to it. You will see, as we already have, that this incredible woman is darn near perfect.

Q: Where were you and how old were you when you first heard that there were men who enjoyed seeing women tied up for pleasure?

A: I first heard it from photographers who work for your company. And that became the first time I experienced bondage—a photo shoot. And I thought, Wow!, this isn't anything like I expected. You see all those movies about guys who want to tie girls up for the sake of being rough with them or worse, and this wasn't that. I never realized what an erotic experience being bound up could be. As I was lying on the floor, sort of struggling, I thought, well, this feels kind of nice. And the next photo shoot, I was struggling around and I thought, this is really nice. I think fetish, including bondage, is healthy since it is just another way to express one's self in a sexual way.

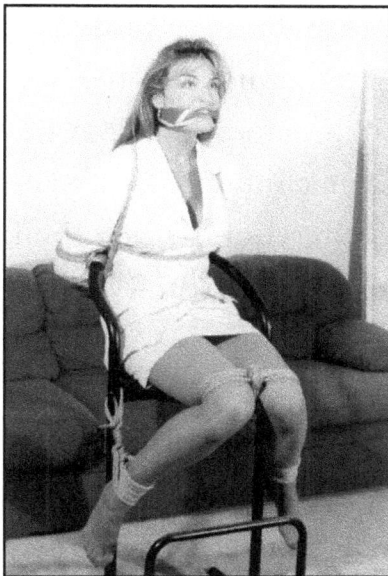

Q: When was the first time you were told that men liked this sight of a

woman tied up? Or had you always known that?

A: Well, my reference was movies and in that case when the man wanted a woman tied up, he was totally psychotic, his intentions were purely evil. Prior to working for you, I had never realized that an individual could tie himself or herself and have an erotic experience.

Q: That must have given you pause about working for a company whose stock-in-trade was visualizations of women tied up—having seen movies in which bad things happened to whoever was tied up.

A: There was some concern. So I asked questions about how extensive it would be, how many people would be present. I checked with my agent, "Have you dealt with these people before?" and he characterized them as just really nice. But I think I exercised proper caution. And your crew really was nice—one called the night before the shoot to ask what kind of juice I would like, what other refreshments. They did everything they could to make me comfortable The first shoot was with Jon Woods and Aaron James and the fact that it was two men concerned me. But immediately it was okay. That was my first video—something about me breaking out of electrical tape. Their behavior and respect caused me to be totally trusting. I eventually wound up working with all of the Harmony people, and I like every one of them. I like the way Chelsea ties because she is very neat, applies just the right amount of pressure and is very fast. I like Jon and Aaron because they do storylines which I think makes the video more interesting and gives me an opportunity to act. And they're fun to joke with.

Q: What would happen if you were out on a date with a man and he confessed that tying you up would be an essential part of his life.

A: I would consider it unusual, not common. It's the way in which he presents it, the reasons he wants to do it, the reason he needs to do it. But I think the bondage itself is totally healthy.

Q: Do you have any reason for why these men like this?

A: Well, maybe a little to do with power but I think it goes well beyond that. She's a Damsel in Distress; she needs me. That's what I get out of it in terms of how you folks do it. He wants to rescue her and that's key.

Q: Could a man who is utterly irresistible to women have this as part of his nature?

A: Sure.

Q: So it's not about a need to have something or someone that you can't otherwise have.

A: No, that would come from negative energy. I see it as a way of expressing yourself, just like certain people enjoy having their hair brushed or feet rubbed and you can't get that feeling from any other activity.

Q: Any common denominators in the men who like this?

A: Physically, no. I haven't come across enough men in my personal life to have a large enough sample to make an accurate statement. It crosses all socio-economic levels, all races, all religions—it's simply physical, something that's in you.

Q: Any idea of where the seed of this might be. Imagine you're a psychiatrist and I come to you and tell you I can't help but have this need to tie up women. What would you tell me is the reason for my feeling that way?

A: Difficult. I might guess that there isn't one single seed - that each man has his own seed - that maybe he saw something when he was a child, maybe mommy and daddy were tying each other up, or maybe he was watching a movie and didn't even realize that he had this craving and it just sort of hit him when he saw it and he thought, wow, that's really erotic. But it would certainly vary from individual to individual.

Q: He saw a movie and if you play that scene out someone rescued her and that somebody was probably a male and by rescuing her earned her undying love.

A: I think when a women can trust a man enough to be tied up by him and when a woman can trust a man and not let him rescue her, there is an innocence in that that's very refreshing, very sweet. We all need that—the older we get, the more purity we need in our lives. It's analogous to longing for that warm safe place to go.

Q: If you were going to produce a commercially successful adult entertainment movie, what are the elements you would put in it to insure its success?

A: I would choose a script that looked good—just like any mainstream movie and instead of having a vanilla love scene, I would have a bondage scene or a scene where the man and woman are getting to know each other. He would rub her feet or suck her toes or tie her ankles, and she has a smile on her face— she likes it. Actually, I would like my movie to include a lot of true fetishes, but be casually presented. For example, if a woman were sitting at a cafe waiting for her lover or husband and she was smok-

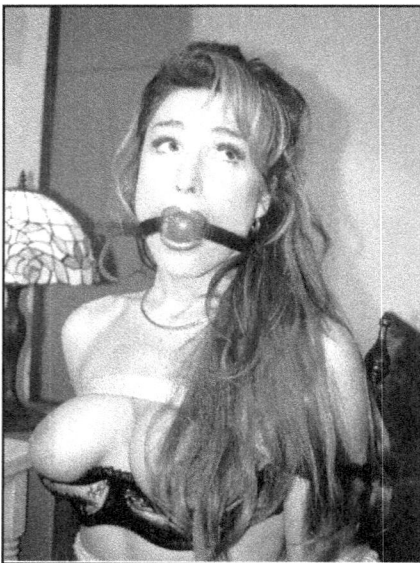

ing a cigarette. I wouldn't just keep a wide shot of this woman smoking a cigarette; I would pan in and linger on the lips and the smoke and then pan out, stay there long enough to get and keep your attention. I think so many people have fetishes, and a lot probably don't even realize it.

Q: What kind of man could win your heart? Men reading this are fantasizing about you as they read this and you are imposing and impressive and they want you to tell them things about them. For example, tell them what they must do to attract your attention, make themselves attractive to you. Not only sexually, but in all ways.

A: There has to be an element of goodness; he can't be a pig. He has to be a good person. A man who is a pig is manipulative—he uses people, men and women. A pig usually has very low self-esteem. A man who is not a pig is not afraid to tell a woman what he wants, not afraid to acknowledge and be comfortable with who he is, and treats himself well.

Q: You would be good at doing this movie because you seem to understand men.

A: I won't say no. I like men very much.

Q: And you like giving the man who is your lover what he needs.

A: True.

Q: Do you understand women?

A: I understand myself sexually, and I understand some women sexually. I'm not bi-sexual, I've never been with a woman. I think women vary greatly in their wants. I would say that my spectrum of erotic taste varies greatly, and maybe there are a lot of women out there whose spectrums are smaller—just kissing, touching. I like that, but I also like a lot of other things. I like fetish because it's like an adult Disneyland— it's

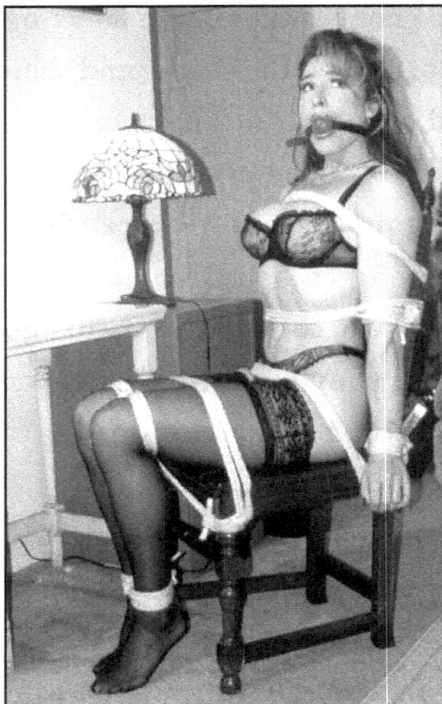

play, it's fun. As fetish grows as it is now doing, including bondage, I think it can become quote unquote the sex of the future since it allows people to be sexual and sensual without actually having sex.

Q: About your man. What does he look like? Is he overweight? Does he dress in a suit or jeans?

A: In terms of dress it's more about mood, since I have a lot of moods. Sometimes I'll want to dress in a cocktail dress and gold earrings, other times I want to wear spandex shorts. Other times I want to wear sweats. So what he wears ought to be a reflection of his mood or where he's going.

Q: Would you date someone who has a beard?

A: I've never dated a guy with a beard, but I did date a guy with a goatee. Guys with beards don't ask me out. But it's not like I wake up in the morning and say, okay, no beards today.

Q: Is he a gentleman? Does he open your door?

A: Yes. He is a gentleman and he enjoys being a man and enjoys being good to a woman—making her feel like a woman - feminine - and appreciating her. I enjoy being a woman, so he should enjoy being a man.

Q: Do you want your man to be stronger than you or equal. Are you willing to be as strong as your man?

A: Yes and no. It depends on the area. I enjoy working and having my own career. And even if I had wealth I would still work because I enjoy working and it feels natural to me. So I'll always have to have my own source of income. I think that women who go after men because of their money are totally evil. I'll always have my own career, so in those terms we'd be equal. We'd be equal in intellect, but in physical strength he should be stronger than I am because I like to be pulled around the house by my ankles.

Q? Do you have wooden floors or carpets?

A: I just slide around on whatever. There are moments when I've been out and I've been talking to attorneys and accountants and photographers and I just want to go home and crash in his arms and he can rub my head and listen to my day and I can just be a little baby.

Q: Do you drink wine?

A: No, I don't drink alcohol.

Q: Does he? Can he?

A: Sure. But he can't be addicted to that or drugs.

Q: Can he be overweight.

A: Sure, I'm overweight. If he's 6'4" and has gained a few pounds I'm not going to freak out. If he starts to gain more I'd try and head him off. So I guess he can't be overweight. But I wouldn't say you've gained fifty pounds and I'm going to break up with you. But I wouldn't just tolerate it either. I think I would poke around and find out what's going on with him, what's causing it. Maybe make suggestions, get him back to rollerblading or playing basketball to get his mind off whatever's bothering him.

Q: If you were to make money answering questions on a certain subject, what subject would best serve you?

A: I spent years studying the chemicals and structure of the brain—physiologi-

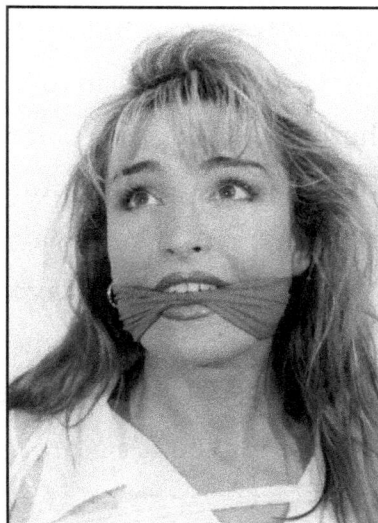

cal psychology, how drugs affect the brain, the links between brain and body, mood and body. That would be a subject I could successfully answer many questions about. It's a path to becoming a psychiatrist or clinical psychologist.

Q: Is that still a goal?

A: It's on the backburner. I initially had the intent of working in this industry for a short amount of time just for financial reasons. But I find I enjoy working in this industry, I enjoy it more than studying physiological psychology. So if I decide when I'm older to go back and get my doctor's, I can do that. So I could probably do well at answering questions about anatomy, psychology, perhaps philosophy. Immanuel Kant is one of my favorites. I'd want to read—philosophers. Poetry, I like Edgar Allen Poe, Sylvia Plath, Robert Frost I enjoy very much—they're all very different, but I like them all for different reasons like a lot of different things in life, different clothes, different music, different books, but I want certain things when I'm in certain moods —.

Q: What is your ethnicity?

A: My mother is American Indian, she's Zuni; my father is German. He lives in Australia, near Perth.

Q: Where haven't you been where you want to go?

A: I'd like to go to Vancouver in Canada. I've met nice people from there and I like the cooler places when I travel. I'd like to go to Alaska. I like nature, animals, taking pictures. When I'm on vacation, I want to get away, really get away.

Q: Do have a favorite bondage position?

A: I enjoy positions where I'm curled up, but not standing with my hands over my head. In terms of position, I think I like everything turned inward, maybe it's a protective thing. I like being in a mummified position.

Q: **Why in your view do some men prefer their tied-up women to be dressed rather than nude?**

A: I think because it contains an element of innocence, and that varies among individuals. I think though a good model never has to take her clothes off; she can transmit her sexual essence through attitude. It's a star quality—it comes from within, you can't fake it.

Q: **There are a couple of other aspects to Harmony's output that we need to acknowledge—spanking and tickling.**

A: I don't want to be spanked. But if it's about spanking someone else, that's okay. I once did spank a guy for a spanking magazine. As for tickling, it's fine. There are certain parts of my body that are very ticklish. Whether or not those parts of me that are naturally ticklish are the same parts the gentlemen want to see me react to may not coincide.

Q: **Who is the most beautiful woman in the world?**

A: Raquel Welch. Her body and her face and her essence transcend time. She's sensual. When she's photographed, it's obvious she's very comfortable with her beauty, her femininity. She doesn't use it like a tool; she's just fabulous. She's on the top of the heap and the heap is very wide. But I like Beverly Johnson, Kim Alexis—high cheekbones, strong jawline, regardless of skin color, hair color, ethnicity, sort of a classic face.

Q: **Let's say it appears that you're about to have a relationship and this new man in your life confesses to you that he**

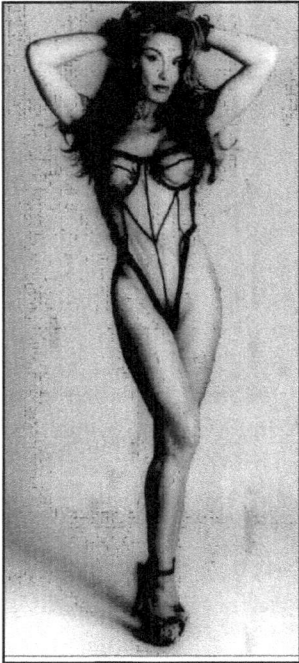

wants to be tied up all the time. How will you feel about that?

A: He never wants to tie me up?

Q: Well, he prefers being the one.

A: I have no problem with tying him up occasionally; that can be erotic. But if he constantly wants to be the one, it's not going to work because I would feel too dominant all the time. There are times when I enjoy being dominant, but I don't want to feel that way all the time. I want to be pursued and tamed and in the female role as well.

Q: Who's the most attractive actor in the world to you?

A: Dolf Lundgren. Solely based on physicality, independent of all other considerations. I think of him in uniform tying me up. I saw Rocky IV and that was it.

Q: Say something if you can to the people who are reading this and liking you and being fascinated by you—say something to make them feel good about that and not ashamed of wanting to see you tied up.

A: Don't be ashamed at all. I like the fact that you enjoy seeing me tied up because I enjoy being tied up. Enjoy my image for as long and often as you wish. Please.

Q: Can we expect to be working with you for a while?

A: Oh, for a long while I think.

Q: Is there any part of this that you don't like?

A: No.

Q: Thanks for spending this time with us.

A: You're welcome.

ONE ON ONE WITH HARMONY SUPERSTAR SHARON KANE

SUMMING UP ALL THOSE SEASONS OF BONDAGE!
By Robert Q. Harmon

Sexuality radiates off this woman like heat off road pavement at high noon.

And not a bit of it is artificial, superficial, deliberate or attempted.

Given what she just naturally has, it isn't necessary for her to lower an eyebrow, undulate a hip, puff up a lower lip or bother with any of the other surface shenanigans women sometimes employ to make themselves sexy.

In her case, any of that would just be superflous. This woman's sexiness is flat-out natural and unorchestrated—finding its bewitching way to the surface from some deeper-within psychic launching pad located not far from her mind and soul.

I had never met Sharon Kane before this interview, even though she had worked on occasion throughout the past few years for the company I own. She's easy to like—affable, kind, unpostured. And she's very introspective— witness her part of the following interview. All the roads that got her to any given moment in her life are lodged in her

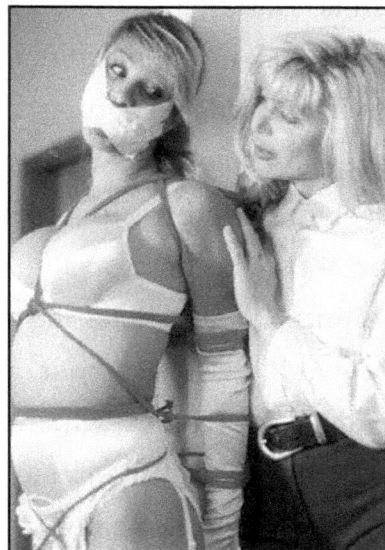

memory like snapshots in a photo-album.

She's in conscious touch with all the barely-perceptible little things that govern her choices and life. Her friends must absolutely treasure her because she is so wonderfully nonjudgmental. Sharon Kane doesn't own a dog or a cat or a bird. She owns a pig named "Candy." Know what? If just one of these things weren't true of her, she probably wouldn't be so dammed sexy.

RQH: Sharon, it's the first time we've met, yet I've been aware of you for some years. When you talk to people, what do you tell them you do...mainstream people...you're at a dinner party with relatives and their friends and they ask you what you do. What's your answer?

SK: My first answer is that I do a lot of things because I do a lot of things and so it prepares them, opens up their minds, gets their minds spreading out instead of they're thinking, oh shoot, she's a secretary. It's changed over the years. I can remember learning to give people that answer when I was doing a lot of adult films. But, before that, when someone would ask me what I did, I would falter and say I was an actress. And the next question, logically, was, well, have you been in anything I've seen? And so, since I wasn't comfortable at that point telling people what I did, I'd say, well probably nothing—just a lot of low-budget "B" movies, which in fact I had done. It didn't take me long to realize that I had an issue here. So why don't

I try do the opposite of what I'm doing now which is overcoming my fear and just saying what it is that I do. So, for a number of years, I practiced telling people exactly what I did and that was very freeing. So now I tell people I do a lot of things, because I do. First, I tell people that I am in the music business because that is my first love and where I'm focusing most of my energy. I tell them I've been in adult films and that I primarily do bondage and fetish work because it's much simpler, much easier, less stressful. I love people; they're very open-minded. And so it works for me to just tell them what I really do. Jeez, if I keep giving you long answers like this, we'll probably only have time for about three questions.

RQH: What do you mean by "people?" Come one, come all?
SK: Whoever.

RQH: Well, who for example would give you pause? Give me the type of person whose reaction you would be concerned about when you're this specific and explicit.

SK: Perhaps If I were dating someone and I met their family, I'd be a little more careful before throwing it out there. In fact, I'm not even sure anymore it's necessary to throw it all out there because I don't need the shock value myself. Sometimes I think it's better to just be discreet.

RQH: What's the worst reaction you've ever had, the most hurtful?

SK: It actually happened very recently. I was at the screening of the Playgirl Centerfold's "Man of the Year." There was an actor there who said, you must be an actress— what do you do...nudies? I said, yeah. I guess he got very uncomfortable with the information, because he then got very nasty and judgmental and really got to me, really hurt my feelings. It still hurts. I was too surprised by his attitude to think of anything snappy to say back to him. I practiced telling people exactly what I did and that was very freeing.

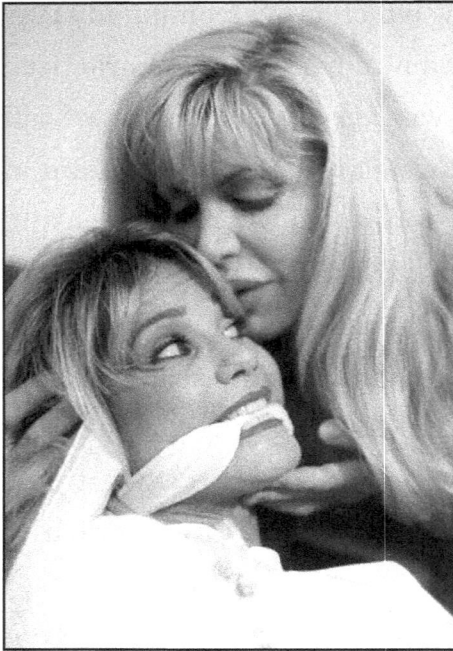

RQH: When you tell people that you're a fetish and bondage actress, those who are most provoked by your answer, what is the question they most ask you?

SK: Provoked in what way?

RQH: Well, they're stimulated by the fact that they've just met this person who does this interesting thing.

SK: They ask if it's real. Are you really hurting people? Are you really having sex with people? They want to know the details of what goes on.

RQH: Are they mostly women, or are they mostly men?

SK: A lot of men. I don't run into that many women. The women I run into are in the business.

RQH: So you don't have a lot of friends outside the business?

SK: I have a lot of friends outside the business, but not a lot of women friends.

RQH: Has anybody ever tried to talk you into getting out of this business?

SK: Sure—boyfriends, ex-lovers.

RQH: Why they in particular?

SK: Sometimes when you hook up with someone outside the business, they feel threatened. They don't really understand the dynamics of it. Somehow they feel it could take away from something I have with them. Being in this business, it's very difficult to have a normal relationship.

RQH: Why?

SK: Well, normal meaning the usual monogamous relationship - "You're mine" and your kind of clutchy, fear-based relationships. People who are together who fear that they will lose their partner or their partner will like another person better. The relationships I have now are based on trust. I don't have typical relationships. I can't because of the work that I do and I like the way my relationships are now because they allow me to be who I am and I can still have intimacy and freedom.

RQH: If you were in love with someone who loved you, would monogamy become one of the essential ingredients of that relationship for you? Is it important to you...fidelity, whatever those words are?

SK: Yes, if that's what happens. It's not something I think is necessary. I think if the relationship were really going and I didn't want to sleep with someone else and that person didn't want to—it's kind of that evolving kind of living. It happens naturally, rather than because one of us is afraid.

RQH: Maybe that's the way it should be with all of us. You put into words something we all wish we felt because it's fair and that's love.

SK: It is love. It is the essence of love to trust because love isn't

something that comes and goes just because someone leaves or comes into your life. Love is something that I think does just exist and that to get to that higher state of love, we all have to go through that. I think it's necessary to release yourself from the attachments and pain that relationships can sometimes bring. It's like walking that fine line in the middle.

RQH: Have you been in love five times in your life?

SK: I would like to think that each time I thought I was in love that maybe I was, but I'm not sure (laughs). I think I've definitely been obsessed and it appears that my obsession has caused me great discomfort at times. I've come to know when I become obsessed with someone, and what I think I've found is that love for me is not being obsessed. It's more open handed because when I get obsessed I want to hold onto something and I want to...

RQH: Rules, fences, boundaries.

SK: Yeah, and I don't want that.

RQH: No freedom.

SK: No freedom. The only way to keep something is to let it go.

RQH: Have you fallen in love with people outside the adult business?

SK: Yeah.

RQH: But of course with that comes that concomitant problem of their being threatened by what you do. You're an object of desire—people see your images in my and other peoples' materials and you become somebody they wonder about. One of the things that men would wonder about you is, what are some of the things you wouldn't like in them, wouldn't care for in a man?

SK: Possessiveness. One who reacts to a situation without think-

ing it through...one who is out of control with his emotions and unable to converse logically about things. Hardcore violence. To me, getting angry and screaming is okay, but I don't think it's necessary. You should be able to communicate your feelings and emotions in a way to get your point across and then resolve it much more quickly than by screaming. So I don't like that.

RQH: Your answer to my next question will make some people happy and others unhappy. Describe your ideal man physically.

SK: It's far beyond that. It's more like the exchange I have with him.

RQH: So he can be short, overweight, baldheaded.

SK: That was my last gentleman.

RQH: Let's get now to the gentlemen reading this magazine. I think they want me to ask certain questions.

SK: Bondage questions.

RQH: I think so. If you met a man to whom this was an overwhelming appetite, a passion, and it was a necessary part of his life. Would that deter you from developing a relationship?

SK: Not at all. No.

RQH; Does that make it more interesting?

SK: Oh yeah.

RQH: You're not telling me what you think I want to hear, I hope.

SK: No.

RQH: He wants to tie you up every night...

SK: Oh, God no—see I have a problem...the tied up part...

RQH: Oh, that's right—you're the lady who doesn't like to be on the receiving end of this.

SK: I don't mind it, but I'm very picky with men who do this. I don't like just any man to do it. It has to be someone I feel pretty comfortable with.

RQH: Because there is an element of danger?

SK: I have some trust issues with men.

RQH: That's fair. But you're saying again that the right man, the right approach, it's really not a problem... you want to develop something with this person before the doors all fly open.

SK: And I guess I shouldn't really say this, but I start to feel kind of claustrophobic and my joints start to hurt.

RQH: Your joints start to hurt? What are you, in your 80's?

SK: Yeah, right. Give me a break here—I have problems with shoulders and neck.

RQH: What if he wants to be tied up? There are a lot of men who privately like that but don't want to concede it. They're fascinated by her predicament, they want to surrender control—the standard stuff that I'm sure you well know. You enter a relationship with a man and he wants to be tied up. Is that off-putting to you?

SK: No, I love that. I think that's really great.

RQH; Why?

SK: Well, because of the nature of men. Look at the world. Men have pretty much been in charge for a really long time. And a lot of men are generally more in touch with their masculine side rather than their feminine side and I think everyone is learning to come into balance. Still, men have a tendency to have to work through all their macho stuff. So I think men being submissive is really a beautiful thing because they're finally relaxing into a passive role, there's more balance to their existence then. I think it's so sexy to feel that softness when they submit to a woman, because the act of submission is such a feminine act.

RQH: You wouldn't care to have your man be this way in all of the aspects of his life though, would you? I shouldn't have put that question that way. What if he were submissive throughout? Submissive to other men in the workplace...

SK: I don't think that's good.

RQH: So you'd like him to have certain masculine traits.

SK: Well, absolutely, because you need strength and you need to be able to stand up for yourself in the world. You have to or you'll get walked over and there are plenty of people to do the walking. I think balance is attractive.

RQH: There is no less a pressure in being a man than in being a woman and you are not acceptable as a young boy if you...that wonderful scene in "Trains, Automobiles" where the John Candy and Steve Martin characters wake up in the same bed realizing that the other person there is not a woman and how threatened they both become and how they respond to the threat by raring up into an outburst of machoism. I think that scene defines beautifully the pressure that men have to be accepted by other men. They can't show weakness. We learn early on to never whine to another man, even a best friend, because it

threatens them. Anyway, how many men have you tied up?

SK: It's in double digits, I guess.

RQH: When you tie up a man, do you tie him the way you want or does he say, do this or do that?

SK: It depends. Beforehand someone lets you know what they like and so you play the little game and that's okay. Of course in a movie, it's all mapped out. If I'm doing it personally, I want to do it the way I want to do it. I'm not cruel. I like sensuality. The element of sensuality being involved with the bondage is important to me. But hurting them?..that's really not my thing.

RQH: Do you fantasize about tying men up?

SK: I just did recently. I actually told the man; he couldn't believe I was saying it. He was shocked. He liked it, but he would never do it. And I wouldn't impose myself on him.

RQH: In your fantasies about a bondage incident in which he's submissive, how's he dressed?

SK: Actually, he's dressed in his suit, so he looks very elegant—white shirt and tie. And I undress him through the ropes. I never really get the clothes fully off, but parts of him are exposed.

RQH: Harmony is producing a few more materials about men being on the receiving end of this just to see if it would be a welcome adjunct to what we've been doing all these years. And the main question we ask is, how

do they want these men dressed...in a suit? do you want them nude?

SK: I guess they become the guy who's tied up rather than becoming aroused by the guy who's actually being tied up. They see the model as a stand-in for themselves.

RQH: How did you learn to be not threatened by the off-beat, unconventional things people do, to be non-judgmental. Where were you raised?

SK: Ohio. Public school. My grandparents raised me until I was 13.

RQH: Why?

SK: My mother and father broke up when I was about a year old. They were both very young and my mother moved us back in with my grandparents.

RQH: Did you go to church, Sunday school?

SK: Yes. I believe in a higher power. I hear voices from time to time that tell me what to do. I feel blessed in that way. I was living in San Francisco in the Haight Ashbury, I was 20. I remember where I was—standing in my bedroom near the kitchen and I heard a voice say, become aware of your judgments. That's when I started internalizing my attention, looking at my thoughts, and when I would meet someone I became aware of an oncoming judgment. And what a judgment looks like—the form it would take.

RQH: How long do you think you'll continue to favor us with your presence in the adult entertainment business?

SK: For as long as I do. If something else happens in the meantime, maybe I'll switch careers. It may be that I'll get too old to do it. One thing I've learned is to never say what my life will be.

RQH: If I look for you in ten years, where will I find you?

SK: I will be strictly writing music. Ten years? That's a way off.

RQH: **Where will you be?**

SK: I see myself over in Europe somewhere. Maybe Spain. I was in Sydney, Australia, about three months ago. That might be promising. I liked that it was very much like America with a European flavor, that it was an English-speaking country. I like that it's on the water and that there's a lot of art.

RQH: Will you miss this business.

SK: No, because when I leave it will be the right time and I'll have something else I love. This will be resolved.

RQH: When is your birthday?

SK: February 24. Pisces, Libra rising.

RQH: Ten years from now, when you no longer miss this business that you're no longer in, but you happen to think back about it, what will be one of the nicer things that you remember?

SK: What comes to my mind first is that I wouldn't be who I am today without it. It's been a major key in liberating my mind.

RQH: Do you think somebody can become over-liberated?

SK: That would become obsession, I think.

RQH: Do you make love to women?

SK: Yes

RQH: If you had to choose between making love to an attractive man and an attractive woman, neither of whom you had ever seen before and purely on a physical basis, which would you pick?

SK: Well since there's no relationship and you're talking about an event whose only purpose is my physical pleasure, I would pick the woman because I trust that she will probably know what to do more than the man because as a woman she would be more apt to be sensitive to another woman's sexual needs. And I think it would be more enjoyable for me with the woman since I would feel safer - you said I had never met either person before — and feeling safer would allow me to relax and enjoy it more.

I'd be too concerned about a man I was meeting for the first time to really let my guard down and allow myself to get into it; he might be rougher than I would want—I'd have to establish some heart connection with him so there could be a romantic evolution.

RQH: In general, do you prefer one or the other gender over the other?

SK: No, but relationship-wise, I tend towards men. I like being in a relationship with men. I'm very physical, I like to go to the gym and work out. To me, it feels very balanced although I love women also. They're two totally different things.

RQH: Who's an actress who might be ideal? Actresses are good references because we all know them.

SK: I don't see women that way.

RQH: So it's not about sexual excitement. Then what is it about?

SK: Admiration, I think. I don't look at a woman and say, God, I've just got to have sex with her. I don't look at men that way either. It's not like that. You admire someone, you respect them. It's more about empathy.

RQH: So, if I were to ask you the same question about a man, I'd get the same answer.

SK: Yep, pretty much so.

RQH: If you were with a man you cared about and you were going to tie him up, how would you tie him?

SK: No set way, it varies depending on the man and the situation and what would seem appropriate at the time. There was an incident that I designed once that you might find interesting. I bought about 20 or 30 lilies and brought them into my bedroom and pulled off those little pollen ends so that the room was filled with the scent of lilies. I lit candles all over the room and spread rose petals over the floor, then went into the kitchen and started making dinner. He arrived and we dined by candlelight and I announced then that I had a surprise for him. I blindfolded him and led him into the bedroom. I made him wait while I changed into a black rubber cat-suit with a zipper in the crotch and openings for my breasts. He was still blindfolded, and I took his clothes off and put leg cuffs on his ankles and attached him to a spreader bar. I tied his hands to an eyehook that I had screwed into the baseboard of the wall. So now he's blindfolded, his wrists are tied and his ankles are parted by the spreader bar and he's lying nude on the floor in a pile of rose petals. The next three hours were unbelievable; I took spectacular liberties. Sure, it sounds carnal and it was. But, more than that, what I enjoyed was the romanticism of the moment—playful and passionate, intensely erotic.

RQH: Further questions fail me, step down please.

SK: If I had to go somewhere for not too long and I had a lover I wanted restrained, I would make sure he was on a feather bed and comfortable, but couldn't get away—I have a great bed for that. His hands are over his head with palms together and his feet are tied with soft rope. When I go away, he's gagged—but when I'm there, he's not because I like those lips at my disposal. He is gagged with scarves and bandannas and he is absolutely nude.

RQH: These last questions were all about someone you like. How would you tie someone you didn't like—someone you thought wasn't very nice?

SK: Handcuffs, cold steel cutting into his wrists! I would tie him to a really hard metal chair with a bright light shining over his face…I'd probably get some lengths of chain and chain his ankles to the legs of his chair. He'd be very uncomfortable, no pity at all for this guy. And he'd be gagged with a huge cock gag so his jaws are splitting wide open and he's drooling all over himself in humiliation. Yeah, that sounds right

RQH: And if I were to ask you those same two questions about women…how you would tie one you liked or one you didn't like?

SK: Exactly as I would a man. But, you know, in the case of nice people, a man or woman I cared about, what I'd really want to do is what they would want me to do. Knowing I was bringing them pleasure would be by far the greatest pleasure for me. And that's really true.

RQH: What are you asked by people who are into bondage? Do they ask you if the sight of someone tied up looks

good to you?

SK: One question I thought you might ask me is the difference between being dominant and submissive. The first time I ever did a bondage movie was in New York. It was okay—I really didn't have any feelings about it one way or the other. I used to go to the "Hellfire Club" a lot—it was a sex club. It was really mixed—straight, gay, bondage, transsexual, everything went on there. Didn't really like it though, because I wasn't into the exhibitionism. But then I came out here and started doing a little bondage with a guy in Long Beach and really hated it.

RQH: Why "hated it?"

SK: I didn't like being tied up by men. And I noticed that whenever I was tied up, a lot of anger would come up. Maybe the fact that I was submitting brought the anger up. Eventually, I started getting cast more in dominant roles and it became a way to express that anger, to turn it around. And since I had done submissive work, I knew what I would not want done to me. I wouldn't do that to people I was with, so it became a way for me to come full circle with the bondage. So after I became a dominant, I just got tired of trying to think of things to say. So then I went the other way and said, Look, if you want to cast me as a submissive, fine. I'm ready to give up control. Like so many other things, it's very cyclical. It was all really good for me because I was able to spend the anger to the extent that I no longer cared which means I had resolved most if not all of the anger. It's a wonderful place to be, and I got that from this because it released me from the need to be dominant.

RQH: At some point in your life, you were a civilian. What is the exact moment in which you stepped into your life as an adult performer? Where were you? How did it happen? Who said what? Where were you working? What were you doing?

SK: I was living in San Francisco and I was working in an Indian restaurant and I hated it. You know, the guy would come up after work and bitch about the water spots on the glasses. I was going to school and studying music and acting. I decided one day when I was playing my guitar and realized that this was my life and I want more time and I want to do what I want to do. In order to have more time to do the little things I want to do, I decided that I would need to find a job that would give me more time. So I answered an ad in the newspaper that said they were looking for dancers and would pay $100 a day. So I went down to the Tenderloin and there was the screening room and I started working there doing girl-girl simulated live sex shows. Most frightening thing I ever did, it was scary, I was totally green. The owner asked me about six weeks later if I'd do a movie.

RQH: What brought you to Los Angeles?

SK : My inner voice. I'd lived in Ohio, San Francisco, Seattle, New York, Montreal. This time, the voice told me that it was time for me to go to Los Angeles.

RQH: At what moment does Harmony become one of the entities in your life?

SK: Simone Devon would call me up and invite me to work and I would drive down and it was always very pleasant and she would do a photo session with me, I think for Harmony. Then I met Mistress Stephanie Locke and we hit it off very well and we would go to her house and do little videos although I don't know if that was for Harmony. But that's how the connection got made. Lately, Chelsea has been calling, so here I am again.

RQH: I imagine you'll work for us a long time because you're very popular with the people who like our materials. Do you have any feelings about these men who adore your pictures

and what they do?

SK: I represent something to each individual. They see something in me that is part of themselves. I couldn't be where I am without them, and they couldn't be where they are without me. And they wouldn't have the outlet to fantasize or be stimulated if I didn't exist. It gives me an outlet too. It's just this one big ball of yarn unwinding. It's a process that they're in and I'm in and we're enabling each other to unravel this ball of yarn and understand ourselves better at the end of it.

RQH: Is what we're all having to accede to that is defined as pornography, does it do the great community of man a disservice and if so, how? Or does it do it a service and, if so, how?

SK: It does both, because the Universe is in the perfect place for it, wherever it is it's fine there, although I think that through trial and error, men and women learn what works for them and what doesn't. And I think that pornography is definitely a way for us to understand ourselves better although not everyone understands that. I grew up in this business, I think that everything I've learned in 20 years or anybody who has been watching explicit material for 20 years can observe their own reactions and learn more about themselves. It's certainly educational, maybe not in the way society thinks it should be because it helps us understand what men like, what women like, helps us live out fantasies that we never would otherwise get to live out.

RQH: What happens when we don't get to act out our fantasies?

SK: Well, it's tragic. But you shouldn't overstep the boundaries—if someone says no, then that means no. But to not express our fantasies because we feel guilty about it just causes problems. It gets bottled up inside and it creates sickness in society because sexual energy is a natural part of life. I think that when sexuality is accepted and expressed, society becomes healthier...the irony here being that in a healthy society the need for pornography would probably be reduced. I think our society is getting more comfortable with pornography. I think it's become more acceptable. That's my take on it after twenty years. It's made me healthy—I don't have any guilt about it or baggage. That's a good place to be. That's the point we want to get to.

RQH: Thank you, Sharon..

SK: You're welcome.

AND NOW THE FINAL SHORT AND SWEET WORDS OF THIS BOOK:

We met about a year ago—involuntarily promoted into a blind date by mutual friends.

His name is Ben and he arranged that we would meet for dinner at a low-key Italian bistro on Melrose, over on the east side of Hollywood. Nice food, low lighting, courteous waiters, Vivaldi in the background. I liked him. He was quiet, unassuming, self-effacing, attentive and polite—easy to take. And, judging from our conversation, I found him worthwhile.

Dinner together became a routine, exclusive of all other date pursuits like movies and concerts and other people's parties. It was like we only had time to learn about each other without interruptions and dinner was the best venue for that. We held hands on our trips to and from his car and we always kissed goodnight. For some reason that didn't seem to bother either of us that's as far as it went even though it was clear we were caring about each other and not seeing other people.

Last Tuesday night, he drove us out of Hollywood and out through the Valley to a small wooded town on a lake. This had a more special feeling than usual. We parked and he led me into a lovely, uncrowded lakeside restaurant. He barely touched his food and, when it was clear that I had finished, he leaned forward and told me what was on his mind and in his heart.

He said he loved me, but needed to tell me secret things about himself that could cause me to not want to see him again, things he had never told anyone else, things that had caused him private shame, things he felt I had a right to know about him. He said he would trust me to never share his secret with another human no matter my own reaction.

And then he told me about bondage—he called it "Love Bondage" – its appeal to him and how he had kept it to himself for a lifetime, not even sharing with people he had loved. When he finished, he sat back with a sad resigned expression, awaiting what I think he assumed would be my denunciation.

I told him I love him. I told him I trusted him and told him that I had heard and read about bondage and, from what I had heard and read, understood that there were men and women who incorporated bondage into their sexual lives as foreplay. I told him that the idea of it hadn't interested me. Until now. I told him I was now very interested.

We are meeting this afternoon at a beachfront hotel. We have reserved a cabana. He has told me that he will bind and gag me and worship and love and that we will stay together forever. I have never been this thrilled before.

And now I ask that you, all of you who are reading this, to wish us your very best.

It is exactly what we wish for you.

Sandra

Definitons

BONDAGE – the state or practice of being physically restrained, as by being tied up, chained,or put in handcuffs, for sexual gratification. A sexual practice in which one partner is physically bound.

Dictionary.com

BONDAGE – sexual activity that involves tying a person up for pleasure.

Merriam-Webster

BONDAGE – considered a fetish, as enthusiasts generally prefer the thought or presence of a fully-clothed restrained partner to a full nude and unrestrained partner.

"Are you willing to try something? Can I tied you to the bed and try a little bondage play?"

Urban Dictionary

BONDAGE – Tying up your significant other with handcuffs as part of a sexual encounter is an example of bondage.

3. The practice of tying people up for sexual pleasure.

"Their marriage broke up when she discovered he had been engaging in bondage games with a local dominatrix while he was supposedly working out at the gym."

Your Dictionary

"I am a dominatrix."
Ladylizdomina